# SECRETS THE MILLIONAIRE MIND

With esteem and admiration, I dedicate this book to youwho believes in the capacity for personal fulfillment and has a millionaire spirit at the bottom of his soul.

## BY EMILY NORA

# Preface

Organizing, planning, saving and building assets are the tests most difficult in an individual's life. It is not for nothing that few manage to conquer this discipline and reach the top. Carlos Wizard Martins, a longtime friend, gathers in this book the wise lessons he learned on his own journey towards prosperity. In gratitude to all he has achieved, with this work he will be able to share his valuable teachings with aspiring millionaires, offering sure guidelines for success, as life is too short to waste it with failed attempts.

I have always believed that if we have a dream, we need to pursue it and do our best to make it come true. My spirit has always been like this: I saw the opportunity and didn't hesitate, put my plan into practice and took a risk. You may fail at some point, but even in a crisis, you learn. In the first chapter, Carlos recounts his experience of being fired at the age of 30 and not knowing which way to go, with bills to pay and family to support. This is really the best way to give us a snap: you have to get out of your comfort zone and be creative, entrepreneurial, think of something big. He started giving private English lessons and suddenly the number of students increased until he found himself with a language school formed. And thus, he became the entrepreneur of the largest franchise chain in the education sector on the planet.

When I was 22, I liked what I did so much and dedicated myself so much to my work that the business started to grow to the point that the agency chartered planes exclusively to take my customers. With that knowledge, I founded my first airline, Morris Air. Soon, Southwest Airlines bought this company that had just appeared on the market and demonstrated an impressive increase in tourist demand. All I did was provide the best possible service to my customers and ensure that the service they purchased was excellent from start to finish. That's the essence: to get amazing results, dream big, think big, have courage and dare to innovate.

Innovation is one of the strongest qualities of an entrepreneur: you either evolve or you don't survive. I recently introduced Live TV at Azul, a system for transmitting live TV programs on board aircraft. I had already tested this service with Jet Blue and saw how important it was to bring this technology to the Brazilian traveler. In Brazil, no one else offers this type of entertainment on board. It remains my personal experience: do not be afraid to do it differently; if you believe, bet. And as Carlos Wizard teaches: success is not a matter of luck, as many people think. Success is preparation, mental attitude, perseverance and discipline.

In short, reading this book awakens the desire to overcome limits, to be what you carry at your core. Glimpse the future you always wanted and determine to reach it as hard as possible. Think about what you can do better than others and do it.

# Contents

# Introduction

In a very early age, I wished to prosper, accumulate wealth and build a fortune. Over the years, I have learned that financial independence, prosperity and success are possible for everyone, but they are not the result of chance. Achievement only happens for those who desire it as much as the air they breathe, and for those who have the discipline to do everything necessary to achieve victory.

I discovered that being rich, prosperous and a millionaire is a personal choice. It is a matter of what you do with your life, and not allowing life to do what it wants with you. It was imbued with these thoughts that I built my entrepreneurial trajectory, raised my family and today I enjoy a full and fulfilling life in every way.

My main motivation for writing this book is to share with you principles, concepts and values that I used both to create a billionaire enterprise and to help train more than a hundred new millionaires in Brazil in recent years.

I want to show how, in a relatively short space of time, I formed Grupo Multi, a Brazilian group composed of ten successful companies, five of which are in the area of language teaching - Wizard, Yázigi, Skill, Alps and Quatrum -, four brands in the professional area

-Microlins, SOS Computers, People and Bit Company -, and a brand aimed at teaching Portuguese and mathematics, Smartz. In all, the group's 3,500 schools serve around 1 million students annually, generate 45,000 direct jobs and are present in ten countries, including the main ones in Latin America, in addition to Japan, China and the United States.

We are the largest franchise network in the education sector on the planet and we are in a constant process of expansion.

"What a lucky guy!", One might think, or else, "He certainly came from a wealthy and powerful family!" No, nothing like that. I was born in a very simple family in Curitiba. My mother was a seamstress and my father, a truck driver merchant. I am the eldest of seven children and at 10 years old I already worked to help my family, selling door-to-door clothes that my mother made. From her, I grew up listening to a phrase that had a big impact on my mind: "To want is to be able". These three magic words were spiced with: "Everything you desire in life you will achieve; dream big; think big".

Since there was no prior wealth, one might assume: "If you left zero and arrived where you arrived, he must be a genius". This is also not true. I consider myself a normal person, I am a Brazilian like you, without any extraordinary characteristics. In fact, in academic terms, I have accumulated a long history of failures: I repeated two school years, I finished high school only at the age of 22 (until today I do not have the courage to show my grades to my children), I entered college late, at 26 years old and I graduated at 30. Shortly after getting my first job, I was fired.

My situation started to change when I discovered the millionaire that was in me. This happened after I went through a situation that marked me a lot (which I will talk about in the next pages) and that made me start what would become the Multi Group. My enterprise, now a billionaire, started in the living room of my house, with a single student, for which I started teaching English. From one student, I started to have two, then three, then a class, two classes ... and what exists today exceeds all my most daring expectations.

However, do not imagine that this trajectory was easy, calm and serene. It was not so, it never is and never will be! The path to success is full of

stones, obstacles and challenges, there are many disappointments, things never work out the first time, and people don't always act as you expect. However, this is the biggest test for anyone who wants to win in any area and the test for anyone who can answer the questions in the affirmative: Am I willing to pay the price to achieve success? Will I do what is necessary, no matter how difficult it is? Will I maintain discipline and a willingness to face any and all adversity until I reach the top?

In general, people who become millionaires have a story of resilience to tell. It was inspired by the overcoming narrated in the American classic The Wizard of Oz (The Wizard of Oz) that I decided to give the name of Wizard to my first English school. In the story, each character carried in his heart a great desire: Dorothy wanted to return to Kansas, the fearful lion wanted to have courage, the scarecrow longed to have a brain and the tin man yearned for a heart. The four walked miles, overcame obstacles, faced great dangers, endured many sufferings until they reached the Land of Oz, to be instructed by the great Wizard.

The wonderful lesson that the magician (Wizard) taught them is that everything they wanted, in fact, already belonged to them: it was enough for each one to explore their own interior. Thus, Dorothy was able to return home, the lion found that he had all the courage he needed, the scarecrow proved to be the most intelligent man in the group, and there could be no more loving person than the tin man.

In the same way that Dorothy and her companions had to take a long journey to reach the Land of Oz, each individual in search of fulfillment needs to travel down the yellow brick road until they reach what they want. Most people would like the conquest to be immediate and without much effort and delude themselves into thinking that life is ungrateful when everything is difficult. He even blames God, saying that He blesses some and punishes others. Don't be fooled: no victory happens by chance. Any achievement, small or large, is the result of the organization itself, the planning itself and a lot of effort.

I hope that this work will help you to build your story of overcoming, personal transformation and financial ascension. My intention is not to teach management practices, economics formulas, market analysis or ways of running a company here. I want to talk about what is going on inside you, more precisely in your mind, in your heart and in your spirit. You will find that wealth, prosperity and success are more related to your mental posture - to your way of thinking, believing and acting - than to tangible factors.

However, I would like to make a reservation: it is not my intention to disparage or belittle those who have few resources. I am not insensitive to their needs and wants and I do not consider the rich better than anyone else. I think this is a personal choice and each one needs to decide, at some point, whether they prefer to spend a life of comfort, prosperity and financial freedom or a life of deprivation.

Many want to succeed, but few have an efficient method of achieving it. For this reason, in the next pages you will learn about the secrets, principles and concepts that I put into practice to, from scratch, achieve a life full of achievements in all aspects. These are the same teachings that have already helped more than a hundred people to become the new millionaires in Brazil.

Be sure of one thing: if I started from scratch, you can start too. If I were able to get out of poverty and move on to wealth, you are also in a position to get there. If I managed to build a fortune, the possibility exists for you too.

Wealth begins within you. Just as the sun does to us every morning, the stronger the light that shines within you, the faster it will awaken the millionaire who is asleep in you.

# Chapter 1

## The bitter taste of failure

The some questions have always intrigued me: why do some people make progress without stopping, while others work hard and can barely pay their bills at the end of the month? Why are some people happy and fulfilled and others dissatisfied and depressed? Why are only a few able to achieve great success? Is having fame, fortune and prestige and being able to accomplish everything you want to be a privilege reserved for a few enlightened ones? Like me, I'm sure you already thought in all of this and more.

That was exactly what was going on in my mind at that critical moment when I received the news that I was being fired. I was 30 years old, I had recently graduated from college, in computer science, saw that my initial goal of making an executive career going down the drain.

That had been my first real job, because until then I had no definite profession, and I had only gotten temporary jobs or underemployment. In addition to this first job, to supplement my income, I taught English at night, at home. He was already married, father of twins, and my wife, Vânia, was pregnant again, waiting for a girl.

The situation was critical, but I still didn't know that that turning point would change my life forever.

If you've had the experience of being fired, you know the feelings that go with it very well. A series of questions circulates in your mind trying to find out why, and especially the "why me?":

Did they not like me?

Did I not do well at work and I didn't even know?

Was it a personal or professional issue?

Is it my way of being, of speaking, of acting?

Do I have no potential?

Will I get another job?

Will it happen again?

Is it just imagination?

Is all this in vain?

Will I be able to go ahead?

Will it be, will it be ...?

In this moment of introspection, we are overcome by feelings of fear, insecurity and an endless number of doubts about ourselves. Then imaginary ghosts arise and make you feel like you're trapped in a small, dark cell. as if, inserted in this prison, you would not be cold or hungry, because you have some clothes and daily you have something to eat. The bed is not very good, but you can sleep reasonably well. The food also doesn't there big deal, but you will survive.

Meanwhile, through the bars, you contemplate the beautiful, wonderful and healthy world outside. You can see others moving around in luxurious cars and living in comfortable homes, and you observe that these people enjoy full freedom of action and expression and work, produce, participate, earn, contribute, love and have fun. And you are trapped there, conditioned to the reality created in your mental state.

All of this makes you feel depressed, marginalized and inferior, because while the whole world thrives around you, you remain trapped between the four imaginary walls and, worse, created by yourself. This condition of imprisonment causes you to revolt, despair, anguish, a deep feeling of sadness and bitterness, which can lead to a convulsive, uncontrollable cry or, even worse, one in which you cannot shed a single tear, but which leaves a pain terrible and a deep emptiness in the soul.

When contemplating the abundant and rich world, in the depths of his being, flashes of hope emerge, who may one day, achieve a distant, remote, and at times almost unattainable happiness. You take a deep breath and start pondering: "How good it would be if I were there! How good it would be if I could have something in life! If only I could be someone ... How fantastic it would be if I could make my dreams come true! ".

When we feel uncomfortable with the situation, at the crossroads that life places us, we are forced to make a decision and follow a new path, because staying in the existing condition is something unbearable as soon as I felt after experiencing the bitter taste of failure and that was the situation I found myself in after that dismissal.

Moments like this are the ideal opportunity to look in the mirror, assess who we really are and contemplate our infinite potential for fulfillment. Often, it is after a great fall that we experience the greatest growth. This is the time to resume projects, renew ambitions and rescue dreams that are sometimes forgotten or asleep in the depths of the soul.

## Dream killers

Dreaming is necessary, but unfortunately most people do not have any kind of enthusiasm, aspiration or ambition. Some even they succeed, but they soon abandon their dreams when they allow themselves to be contaminated by negative and critical comments from the "dream killers", who are often good and well-intentioned advisers, but who, due to their inability to fight for their ideals, manage to convince them that your dream is impossible and that you will never realize it.

Generally, "dream killers" tend to use their free time for useless activities, with no purpose or direction. Thus, they do not need to focus on the pursuit of self-realization and try to convince you to do the same. Unfortunately, some talented people let themselves be influenced by these negative comments and end up abandoning their goals of prosperity, thinking that life is just like that.

There are also the "dream killers" who hope for your failure and are happy to see you in a bad condition, because that way they justify themselves with the false sense of equality in the midst of mediocrity. And sometimes, when you're sick, they help you feel even worse.

You then postpone your plans. Perhaps you have already postponed your goals and dreams so many times, that you are even tired. However, his thought does not give him peace of mind and continues to charge him incessantly: "What about that dream?

What are you going to do with it? " You pretend not to hear, just nod and say: "oh, I know, that dream, I'm thinking about it". A few days pass, you dream more. Sometimes he wakes up at night, he cannot sleep, he turns from side to side in bed, and the question continues: "Have you forgotten your grand dream?" "No, I haven't forgotten, I'm always thinking about him".

Then, you try to change the subject. He fails and ends up answering: "it's fine. This week I cannot think about it, I am very busy at the company, it is the end of the month. I need to work until 8 o'clock at night. When I get home, I can barely dine and watch some television. At these times, I am already tired with exhaustion. I often end up sleeping on the couch. For those who struggle so much during the week, the weekend is just for shopping at the supermarket and watching television ".

So you make a deal with yourself: "As soon as I pass this phase, I promise to stop everything just to plan how I will realize my dream of getting rich. It's okay like that?".

That way, you spend another month, another semester, another year postponing, postponing, postponing the realization of your great dream of prosperity. In fact, you are postponing the great journey within yourself, which is the place where things need to happen first, before they can materialize in your life. As long as you don't stop everything to align your mind and heart with the laws that generate wealth, you will continue to suffer the consequences of this dichotomy of wanting something great and spending your days suffering and regretting the existing reality.

# Self-imposed defeat

Whether it is your current condition of abundance or misery, it reveals exactly your most intimate desires and beliefs. Someone may then think, "I never wished I was in the bad situation I find myself in." To understand why people live in unfavorable conditions, think for a moment that there is a wasteland next to your house and imagine how good it would be if that land naturally produced strawberries, oranges, apples and grapes. It would be wonderful to be able to pick up these fruits in the morning to enjoy them with pleasure.

However, this never happens. What do you usually see on vacant lots? Weed, thorns, dirt, filth, snakes, mice, diseases, danger etc. If the land is abandoned, it is a sign that nobody has planted anything, and this is a universal law: you only reap what you plant, care for and water, and nothing else.

The same is true on the stage of your mind. If it is not cultivated with principles of prosperity and high ideals, it yields to poverty, failure and misery.

I once heard the following statement from a person who seemed well-intentioned and sincere: "I am not an ambitious person, I do not desire luxury, elegance, sophistication". This comment may seem absurd and even false, but it is a genuine picture of the thoughts of thousands of people who hypnotize themselves with feelings of self-pity, trying to deceive themselves, claiming that they do not want to obtain what they would most like to have.

Unconsciously, they suffer from self-imposed defeat, because, in addition to not wanting good for themselves, they spend their energies trying to attract the effects of a negative mental attitude. Therefore, understand that your current social condition reveals your deepest desires.

## Fear of prospering

It may seem incredible, but unconsciously some people carry enormous fear within them: they are afraid to prosper and accumulate wealth. "How can anyone be afraid of getting rich?", You may ask. And I say that this fear is real, common, and it is one of the main reasons why many fail to progress financially.

These people live like this: "If I get rich, I will be robbed, kidnapped, maybe killed. Not counting the number of people who are going to knock on my door to borrow money ". Seized by a terrible feeling of fear, they hypnotize themselves, and accept financial failure as a permanent condition. They cannot imagine any different scenario, apart from their state of uncertainty, insecurity and instability.

Generally, people who think this way are justified like this: "My grandparents were poor, my parents were poor, I was born poor, I am going to die poor". They live as if they were predestined to spend an existence of suffering, anguish and afflictions. Some people even accept this condition unfavorable, as if it were some design or divine will, when in fact there is no virtue in poverty. It generates hunger, malnutrition, disease, illiteracy, intrigue, confusion, concerns, disagreements, crying, irritation, ulcers, misfortunes and does not benefit anyone. I am sure that not even God is happy with misery.

Poverty is an anomaly existing within man, in his way of thinking and acting. The belief held by many that poverty reveals the purity of the individual has no scientific, psychological or spiritual basis. In my opinion, this is just a rationalization created by those who chose the path of least resistance.

The famous writer Helbert Hubbard described very clearly the reality of the lives of thousands of men and women who deceive themselves, consciously or unconsciously, every day. They belong to the large crowd and are considered ordinary individuals, with no objective to follow, they do not miss work, but they do not have urgency in their actions, they do not commit themselves to dates, deadlines or results and need to be reminded at all times of their obligations. Some spend their hours hiding, dodging, killing time until it is time to leave.

Unhappy with this situation, he wrote: "Every successful entrepreneur faces the challenge of the common man, unable or unwilling to concentrate on a task and carry it through. Foolish and irritating inattention and sloppy work seem to be the general rule. The inability to act independently, the endless inertia, the unwillingness and the reluctance to engage happily in a work are the causes that place the well-being of the crowd in an increasingly remote future. Unfortunately, many people do only the minimum required to avoid being fired at the end of the month. If men do not have the initiative to act for their own benefit, what will they do when the result of their effort results in the benefit of all? "

In reality, some people always look for excuses, attributing to their circumstances their failure and their unsuccessful situation. Next, I'll talk about the most common excuses for those who have failed to succeed or create fortune.

# Chapter 2

## The seven deadly excuses

The now you will know the seven deadly excuses of people unsuccessful. They are called mortals because each of them has the power to destroy dreams, end the mood and kill the hopes of daysbest.

The carrier of this contagious virus has symptoms of constant nervous crises, brain disorders and acute pains of conscience. If not treated in time, you can suffer serious professional complications, which can be fatal, in extreme cases.

To protect yourself from this evil, you should get vaccinated and stay away from any individual already infected by the virus, as it is highly contagious, coming from people dominated by failure. And you need to get vaccinated, protecting yourself from what people say, who, every day, keep success from themselves.

Sorry 1

# Here nothing goes right

First, unsuccessful people do not believe in the place where they live, in their own city, state or country. They are always saying to themselves and to others: "This city is not a good one. Everything that starts here does not go ahead. There are no opportunities here. I've tried everything, but nothing worked. If it were in the capital, it would be different ". The unfortunate individual in the capital

says exactly the opposite: "The problem is the big city. Everything already exists here.

This city has a lot of people. If I were in the country, it would be different ".

These individuals are always looking for an excuse and do not take responsibility for their actions. They unconsciously desire to be elsewhere and always seek an external reason to justify their internal surrender. While the defeated change cities and run away from themselves, the victors progress both in the countryside and in the capital. This reality reminds me of a story:

There was a traveler who, arriving in a certain city, asked a resident: "What is this city like?" O

resident answered him with another question: "What was the city where you came from?". And the traveler replied: "My city was not a good one. The people there were proud, greedy, envious, negative, pessimistic, they did not like to work, they criticized each other and found excuses to justify their mistakes ". The resident replied: "This city is just like yours".

The traveler thanked him and went on his way. Another traveler approached this resident and asked him the same question. Again, he asked her what the old city was like. The second traveler replied with a smile, saying that his city of origin was very good, people were friendly, honest, hardworking, positive, optimistic, hospitable and always tried to help each other. The resident then said: "You are going to love this place. The people here are the same as those in your city ".

Sorry 2

## The competition is very big

Some give the excuse of competition, whether in the academic, professional or business areas. They often say: "Nowadays there are many lawyers, doctors, dentists, engineers, therapists, psychologists, teachers, etc." They forget that there are renowned, respected and successful professionals, and others without a name, without prestige and strangers.

Some people who work in large companies often say: "Here it is very difficult to move up the career ladder. The structure is already well defined ". These people reason as if their work is invisible and

it didn't matter. In fact, the larger the company, the greater the opportunity for the individual to grow and progress, as the professional's performance has a great impact on the organization's profit. For this reason, those who stand out will always be observed and admired by a greater number of people.

The false entrepreneur with an apologetic mind thinks like this: "It is better not to open a business here. There is already a lot of competition in this area ". Personally, I have always found it interesting to open an English school where there are many competitors, as this demonstrates that the education sector is an excellent business, because, otherwise, they would all be broke.

Some would-be entrepreneurs, infected by this excuse, claim: "Competitors are dominating the market". And I say: congratulations to them, because they are working in the right way, because dominating the market must be the goal of every entrepreneur. The professional who is intimidated by the competition is only declaring his unwillingness to meet the needs of internal or external customers, whether in the organization for which he works or to adapt to the demands of the market.

I have always admired the competition, it stimulates creativity, generates ideas, forces us to restructure the company, leads to dismissing incompetents, offers better salaries for the qualified, hires better professionals, generates more resources, invests in advertising, promotes training and better serves the client.

Therefore, competition can be both a stimulus for professional overcoming and a great excuse for not taking action. Be careful that she doesn't get you out of the game.

Sorry 3

## You have to pay a lot of taxes

There are people who use the excuse of Brazil's high tax rates in an attempt to justify their professional and business inertia.

How many people do you know who, having a good commercial activity, with good prospects, simply say: "I cannot grow. If I grow up, the government will take all my money. I will also need to hire more employees and, you know, the charges and labor laws in this country are absurd. So it is better to leave the business as is ".

Sometimes, in a company, we find people who even prefer to earn less, just to avoid paying the taxes resulting from a higher remuneration.

The virus of this excuse is very dangerous, as it exposes not only the small mentality of its bearer, but reveals other symptoms even more serious, such as envy, selfishness and meanness. People infected with this virus still need to learn the "win-win" concept. They usually think that someone needs to lose in order for them to win.

These people are poor in spirit, as they would like the result of their work to benefit only themselves and no one else. They have no sense of social responsibility for the community, the community or the neighbor. In fact, they feel pain in their soul when they know that someone will benefit from their work. They often say: "They want to win at all", and with that thought, they prefer to deprive themselves of the benefits of their own efforts rather than share a portion of their earnings with their peers, with the institution or with the country.

## Lack of money

Some "apology experts" claim that people are currently broke and that there are only three ways to get rich: receive an inheritance, win the lottery or marry a rich person. In reality, there has never been a more prosperous time in this country's recent history when people have access to imported cars and so many other consumer goods.

In fact, only those who complain about the lack of money are without money. All the others are doing well, thank you. It is not because you are experiencing difficulties that the whole world is like you. If that were the case, the stores, the banks, the streets would be empty, there would be no trucks on the roads, no planes would take off or there would even be no newspaper or television. Such people look at the world through binoculars in reverse. For them, objects are much further away than they are in reality.

Sorry 5

## There are crises and uncertainties

Whoever gives this excuse says that today everything is very risky, as we are experiencing political uncertainties and crises around the world, and the moment is not ripe for the opening of new businesses; so it's better to wait for a definition to see how things are going to look.

Whoever makes this excuse may have been the victim of many economic crises in the past and has yet to recover emotionally. People like that say: "The global financial system is on the verge of total collapse, we live in a dangerous globalized economy, in which a tsunami in Japan can cause a financial tsunami on the other side of the world. The United States is facing its biggest financial crisis, Europe is broken and China wants to take over the world. Markets are going through a phase of unprecedented uncertainty, large banks and traditional companies are closing their doors, unemployment is rising everywhere and not even experts can predict whether there will be an even bigger financial crisis. For all these reasons,

Whoever speaks in this way forgets that while there are individuals going bankrupt there are others making a fortune; there are economies in recession and there are emerging economies. For the pessimist, it does not matter the condition of economy, when faced with an opportunity he will always see a crisis, while the optimist, when faced with a crisis, will always see an opportunity.

# I'm not lucky

There are those who think that success is a matter of luck and opportunism. Some go months without work and justify themselves by saying: "I'm out of luck. I can't find a placement in my area ". These people tend to look at the success of others with jealousy and envy and, in a tone of contempt, say: "For so-and-so everything works out. He was born with the star ". Others still think that "every rich person is a thief, corrupt and a profiteer".

Thus, they ignore the long hours of preparation, the choices and the consequences, the wrong and right decisions, the corrections of course along the trajectory and believe that their successful neighbor never faced adversity.

Those who think of bad luck do not know that 70% of young people who graduate do not find jobs in their area, but they manage to succeed when they break the cycle of unemployment by taking any job and then looking for a better placement.

The classic writer James Allen described these people as follows: "Some, seeing a man doing well, observing only the positive effects of his achievements and ignoring the process itself, say:" Here's a lucky guy. " Such people do not take into account the trials, failures and struggles that man faced in order to gain the experience; they do not recognize the sacrifices he has made, the courageous efforts he has proposed, the faith he has nurtured to overcome the seemingly insurmountable obstacles in order to be able to fulfill his great dreams. They do not see the long and arduous journey, they do not know about the darkness or the sadness they faced. They see only the light, the beauty and the joy of the objective already accomplished and they call it luck ".

In addition to claiming their bad luck, there are those who despise the "luck" of the rich. They just don't realize that thinking like that they will never become millionaires. How can someone become something he despises? This is impossible.

## Sorry 7

The seventh excuse is the most dangerous of all. I did not write it here because each person knows her well, since she has been living with her for years, who is her "friend and faithful companion". It is the reason that everyone claims that they are not yet prosperous and very successful.

I don't even need to know how each one would fill this gap, but one thing I'm sure of: this excuse that you give to yourself comes from your conformism. You have settled for it and believe that things are just like that and will not change.

The side effect of this excuse is serious, and treatment is very difficult, as your body has probably created antibodies to defend itself against it. The ingrained conformity in you eliminates your initiative, kills your creativity, buries your talents, puts an end to the hope of better days and makes you a victim of circumstances.

Sometimes, conformism is so deeply ingrained in the human being that he cannot easily eliminate it. Only through a lot of personal effort and adequate help are people able to overcome false concepts, usually acquired during childhood and youth because of the environment of excessive deprivation and deprivation.

In reality, anyone who wants to walk the road of success cannot be bound by excuses. There is no such thing as "life didn't smile for me" or "life was cruel to me". If you want to become prosperous, you must heroically decide to face the mirror and say goodbye to your old self in order to embrace a new way of being, without blockages, complexes and excuses.

If you want to turn your life around, you need to make a serious decision, the result of deep analysis and frank conversation with yourself: you need to decide to awaken the millionaire in you. Thus, you will know a new self that is rich, prosperous and has the millionaire spirit itself. When you hug him once and for all, you will see that he will become your greatest ally.

# Chapter 3

## In search of prosperity

My resignation, despite signaling a very difficult situation, was the watershed for the resumption of my dreams and goals.

At that time, I knew I had two choices: I could look for another job and try a new job in another company or do what I wanted and dreamed of: setting up my business and undertaking.

In reality, it was not just my dream. It was already ours: mine and Vânia's. We started dreaming together from the day we got married.

Although Vânia and I had known each other since adolescence, we only started dating when I was 22 years old. I was taking a supplementary course, because I wanted to finish high school, since I had the hope of one day passing the entrance exam, getting a good job and starting a family. She was beautiful, talented and wonderful, and after a month-long "long" courtship, I proposed to her, which happened after just ninety days. I'm sure she accepted it out of pure love and innocence, because at the time she earned two minimum wages per month, and I, one.

Everything was very simple: the wedding invitations were photocopies, the photos were taken by a friend and the sweets were made at home. After the ceremony, we left for the honeymoon in a van loaned to Camboriú, in Santa Catarina. One night, sitting on the beach sand, in a moment of inspiration, we set some goals for the future. One of them was unforgettable: we will seek prosperity.

We came back to face the life of newlyweds, not knowing what to do to get out of poverty and achieve wealth. We were unable to conceive, at that moment, the immense obstacles and barriers that we would face in the search for self-sufficiency. We were not sure what it meant to be successful and what the implications of this unknown world were. We had no map, script or guide to follow, we only had the strong desire, the hope and the confidence to build a great fortune.

## When preparation finds the opportunity

I knew that if I wanted to change my financial situation, I would need to change my academic condition first. With that goal in mind, for three years my wife and I worked and saved enough so that I could attend a university, not in Brazil, but in the United States. At the time, I was already fluent in English, as I had learned the language of Shakespeare in my teens from the young Mormon missionaries who always visited my home.

With my own effort, family support, and encouragement from Mormon church leaders, I was able to be accepted at Brigham Young University in Utah, USA. In that excellent academic environment, I studied computer science and statistics and, at the same time, I had the opportunity to work as a Portuguese language instructor for foreigners at the university's language center. After graduation, I was hired by Champion International, in Cincinnati, where I worked for a year, and was later transferred to the Brazilian branch, in Mogi Guaçu, SP.

As a recent graduate, at the age of 30, my main goal was to make a career as an executive. He imagined working in several companies and moving up the corporate ladder towards professional success.

I have always believed that success happens when preparation finds an opportunity. One day, I was at work when a colleague told me

asked, "Could you give me some English lessons at night?" I thought so: English classes mean more money in your pocket, and that doesn't hurt anyone. And I did.

I then started to teach in the living room of my house at night. After that my first student, another one arrived, and then another one and another ... In a short time, I was teaching classes for a class, then for two, three ... After a few months, my wife also started to teach in home and, as time went by, the number of students increased.

At that time, English classes were nothing more than a supplement to family income. It is interesting to note that sometimes we have a gift, a talent, a natural ability, but we ourselves cannot recognize it immediately, and that happened to me.

I worked at Champion during the day, gave classes at home at night and continued to look for a solution: "Where will I find success? How can I be successful? What to do to win financially? Will I always be an employee or can I be an employer? ".

The solution was before my eyes, but I still couldn't see it. While thinking about all that, one day I went to the bank to receive my salary. When I was in the checkout queue, I noticed that on the counter there was an open folder with the title "Payroll - Confidential". I looked well and saw that it was from the company I was working for worked!

When it was my turn to be answered, I stretched my eyes and saw that the first name on the list was my boss's. He was a professional with twenty years of career, who had already worked in large companies and had an impeccable resume, but, to my surprise, when I noticed the value of his salary on the list, I was a little surprised. I then asked the cashier girl, "Is this payroll monthly, biweekly or weekly?" She laughed and said, "Of course it is monthly. The company does not make biweekly or weekly payments

Then I received my humble salary and went home unhappy. I didn't believe it! I thought that a director's salary was higher, but much higher.

So I evaluated: do I want to work another twenty years and then earn this remuneration? Am I willing to submit to all the demands of corporate escalation so that, when I get close to retirement, get a check like that? Wouldn't I be able to make bigger gains if I worked on my own?

## The decision to get rich

With the experience I have today, I can safely say that if you want to be well, have a peaceful and comfortable life, you must work for a good company. You will have a beautiful house, a nice car and you can take a trip to the beach from time to time.

However, if you want to have a superhome, a supercar and travel all over the world, if your intention is to become rich, very rich, millionaire or multimillionaire, you will need to undertake, open your own business and learn to multiply your talents and resources.

That experience in the bank queue gave me a sense of definition and purpose. I clearly felt that the path to prosperity consisted of the entrepreneurial capacity of each one. Although I still didn't know what my life project would be, at that moment I decided that I would be an entrepreneur and earn my living by developing my own plans, goals, objectives, and would earn more or less in proportion to my efforts.

To put this objective into practice, for a while, I would need to keep that job of mine in order to be able to cover the expenses of the month until I can establish myself with my business. As long as this did not happen, it would be foolish to ask for the termination of the company. In my heart, however,

incomprehensibly to myself, there was a still, small voice that said:

You can do more!

Believe in yourself!

Believe in your dreams!

Even so, while I wanted to believe in the inner voice, I thought:

But what will it be like when I quit my safe job?•

Is it•really worth abandoning the stability and security of fixed employment?

Am I going to take a risk without even knowing what business I'm going to open or in what area I'm going to operate?

What will my wife think of all this?

What will my parents' reaction be?

What will others say?

What if I fail?

And if everything goes wrong?

As I tried to fight those negative voices and keep the flame burning to become an entrepreneur, I felt like I had a thousand-piece puzzle in my hands to put together. It was as if the pieces were all loose, spread out on the table, but there was no image, photo or illustration on which to base myself. I just knew that I would have my own business and nothing else.

In an attempt to define in which area to act, I remember having made with my wife a list of ten possible projects, which varied in size, nature and segment. Faced with the diversity of options, for a time I felt totally disoriented, not knowing which path to follow, which way to go and where to start.

He also knew that in any area he was going to act, it would take a long time to obtain a satisfactory financial return. Possibly, in the beginning, I would receive nothing or almost nothing. If he received enough to support the family, he would be satisfied. I also knew that I did not dominate the operation of any of the ten listed businesses.

In that moment of uncertainty, I had the distinct feeling that I needed divine inspiration, an orientation superior to my intellectual capacity, to help me make the right decision, because it would not be just any job or business, but a project of life. It would be a cause, an ideal for which I would do my best, because I was willing to dedicate all my energy, my gifts and talents to the success of the enterprise.

Although I didn't know which way to go or where to start or how to proceed, within me there was a certainty: that God knew and He could tell me which way I should go.

An answer Imbued with that spirit, I remembered a very inspiring scene from a film that I really liked: A violinist on the roof. This anthological film tells the moving story of Tevie and his family, who lived in a terrible state of poverty in ancient Russia.

The film portrays the saga of that Jewish family towards the security, stability and comfort of America. The protagonist, Tevie, raised cows and sold milk with his cart in the village of Anatevka. At a certain point, his horse gets sick and he starts to pull the cart to deliver. Very dejected and unhappy with the situation of need he faced, he stops on the way, looks at the heavens and, very moved, begins a dialogue with the Creator: "My dear God, what would happen if I were a rich man? What would happen if I had a fortune? Even if it was a small fortune, would it ruin your plans? ".

I felt exactly like Tevie: with a wife and small children to raise, living in great poverty, in a state of deprivation and, at the same time, dreaming of "making America" even after I have already returned from there.

In the same spirit of prayer, I decided to repeat the sequence of questions asked by Tevie and added: "My Heavenly Father, what path should I follow that will provide me with the greatest personal, professional and financial fulfillment? What profession should I perform to help me satisfactorily fulfill the purposes of my existence? How should I apply the divine talents and gifts that the Lord has given me, even though I am completely unaware of what those gifts are? How can I generate wealth for myself, for those around me and for society in general? ".

Suddenly, an unforgettable feeling took over my heart, my mind and my spirit. The answer was quite clear. At that moment, I felt that I should follow the area of education, the area of teaching, the area of training people.

As soon as that thought crystallized in my mind, the next question I asked was, "But how am I going to do that?" And the silent answer was: "Ask and you will receive, seek and find, knock and it will be opened to you".

After that memorable moment, there were no more questions, doubts or uncertainties about which direction to go. I knew, however, that I had a huge dark tunnel to go through. I discovered that when we are in an inner search, following the spirit of "ask and you will receive, seek and find", at some point, we need to take a step in the darkness and trust only in faith. It is as if God were placing us in front of a dark tunnel with enough light to cover just one or two meters, however, as soon as we walk on this route, we soon receive a new beam of light of another one or two meters.

Having received that divine inspiration made all the difference in my personal and professional trajectory, because I knew that, at any moment, I

he could turn to the same source of inspiration for support, comfort, encouragement and direction. That answer also gave me more certainty, confidence and strength to persevere on the path to be taken.

Coincidentally, a few weeks after receiving this response, my boss called me into his office for a quick chat. He explained that the company was undergoing a restructuring and that my name was on the list of employees to be fired. He didn't give me many explanations and just asked me to gather my personal belongings, saying that I didn't need to go back to work the next day.

Yes, today I know that that same dismissal that ended my so-called executive career was the way the universe found to say to me: "Now it's time for you to move on towards the lonely path of prosperity. Move on. Your time has come! ".

That period when I was able to work as a professor at the language center of the American university was, without my knowledge at the time, as an important stage in my professional qualification.

And those English classes at my home were the embryo of the emergence of the first Wizard school in this country and the first building block for the Multi Group, which would become the world's leading company in bilingual education.

Who knew that that teacher who started teaching at home would one day be invited to accompany the President of the Republic, Dilma Rousseff, on her visit to China? Who could have predicted that that project would become one of the largest educational groups in the country?

When I contemplate all these achievements, I often remember the words of the English author Robert Frost: "There were two roads in the woods. At one point, they separated. I took the road less traveled, and it made all the difference ".

The seven golden keys to prosperity

Today, I am fully convinced that we can achieve everything we desire. After realizing my dream, I can say that what helped me to succeed were some fundamental aspects, which I decided to call the seven golden keys and I will share with you on the following pages. The 7 golden keys to prosperity helped me transform an amateur and domestic activity into a multi-million dollar enterprise.

In the same way that I managed to leave that imaginary cell created by myself in the past, it was your turn. I will put the keys that open the cell doors in your hands. It is your opportunity to open the heavy and rusty door that imprisons you and run free to the world of your dreams.

The time has come for you to awaken the millionaire in you.

**To awaken the millionaire in you, remember:**

Success happens when preparation finds the opportunity. So get ready and be aware of what is happening in the world and around you. If you want to be well, work for others.

If you want to get rich, work on your own.

**Mentalize:**

Prosperity is in me.

I can do more, much more.

There is a millionaire inside me.

# Chapter 4

## Golden key 1
## Zero your past

D egrees in your mental and emotional attitude.

If, due to lack of experience, over the years you have taken out loans, made commitments that you have been unable to settle and have accumulated an undesirable history of defaults, you will need to take a new stance towards yourself, your family and society in order to be able to get rid of these currents, which enslave him for so long, deprive him of sleep and peace of mind.

As long as you do not get rid of these financial bonds, you will remain an individual stuck in the past and will not be able to progress. I am going to report an experience I had with a person who managed to pay off his debts held for years, the source of which was purely emotional.

At the beginning of my business trajectory, we had a very interesting franchised client. He was a mature, experienced and apparently successful businessman. It had a beautiful school, with great facilities and well-trained teachers, its classes were quality and its students were satisfied. This franchisee was exemplary in all

the senses: investing in marketing, promoting cultural events, performing extracurricular activities, etc. He had only one problem: he never paid his bills on time. He paid for them only after receiving many calls, charges and warnings.

When analyzing the situation, we found that the problem was not a lack of money, as he had a beautiful house, a good car, a great financial movement and always had the resources to travel with his family. The question was different.

He once came personally to the company's headquarters and, despite his negative credit, wanted to place an order, which was obviously refused. Then he asked to speak to me and I promptly answered it. After listening to his long speech that tried to justify his default, I said to him: "My friend, allow him to say something that you already know. The reason you don't pay your bills is not a lack of money. You don't pay your bills because you don't want to pay them ".

Then I added: "If you allow me to be more frank, I can explain something more to you. In my opinion, during your childhood or adolescence, you probably must have suffered some kind of psychological trauma, and the negative situation of yesteryear ended up now manifesting in your adult life. Therefore, you try to take advantage of someone, thinking that it will make up for the suffering of the past. You have been doing this for so long that you have even gotten used to it, and now you accept this practice as something normal ".

I ended my comments like this: "As I have great respect and admiration for you, I would like to recommend you some great courses carried out by competent professionals, who will be able to help you overcome these unresolved emotional situations of the past."

He listened carefully to my words. At the end, he asked: "What about my order? Will it be released? ". I replied: "Yes, he will be released. You just need to settle the pending amounts and you will be released immediately.

To my surprise and, certainly, to his surprise too, he ended up paying the amounts due and returned home with his request granted. And the most surprising thing was that, from that moment on, he never delayed his payments again.

There are some curious cases. There are some people who, even though they are able, do not pay their debts, motivated by a spirit of revenge. They act as if their improper behavior were able to repair or to think about an adverse situation experienced in the past. They retain the feeling that someone owes them something, no matter who it is. Some think they are the parents, the brother or sister, the husband or wife, the company, the boss, the country, the government and even God.

Others increase their debts motivated by envy. Regardless of their financial capacity, they think: "If my neighbor changed his car, I will also change it. If my friends are going to travel abroad, I will also travel. If my friends buy this brand of handbag, I will also buy it ". These people live by comparing themselves to others. Thus, they suffer, as they will always find someone in a more privileged condition than yours.

There are also the poor in spirit, who do not honor their commitments and justify themselves by saying: "My creditors already have so much, and I have so little. If I don't pay that bill it won't make a difference to them ". From a financial point of view, the amount owed may not make much difference to the creditor who has infinite wealth within him. However, unfortunately, the lack of payment makes all the difference in the life of the debtor, who, due to his condemnable attitude, ends up attracting more financial, emotional and physical discomfort to himself.

People like that still need to learn the age-old concept that "everything that comes out of you will return to you". If goodness, charity and generosity come out of your heart, these gifts will multiply in your life. On the other hand, if you cause harm, damage, misfortune to others, these

annoyances, sooner or later, will return to you. Thus, it is wrong to believe that, by failing to pay their debts, they will disappear. On the contrary, they will only increase. After all, those who understand interest receive, those who do not understand pay.

Notice what wise educator J. Reuben Clark Jr. said about interest bondage: "Interest never sleeps or gets sick or dies; they never go to the hospital; they work on Sundays and holidays; never go on vacation; never visit or travel; they do not take time for leisure; they are never without work or unemployed. Once in debt, interest is your companions every minute of the day and night; there is no way to avoid them or escape from them; you cannot ignore them and whenever you fail to meet their demands, they will crush you ".

Recently, a friend came to me very enthusiastically. He said with a huge smile on his face: "I am feeling so good, so relieved, so confident". "What happened?", I asked him. And he confided to me: "After five years, I managed to pay off all my debts and clear my name." "My congratulations on this victory, but how did you manage to do that?", I asked. His response moved me: "I couldn't take this weight anymore and I decided to make any necessary sacrifice to get rid of this burden. For you to have an idea, in the last few months even my food stamps I sold so I could pay off the debts ".

There is no middle ground in the pursuit of prosperity. You are the one who decides at every moment how to handle your money, how to control your expenses, reduce your expenses, allocate your resources and pay off your debts. Daily, you are approaching or distancing yourself from wealth. It's your choice. And it is the small daily choices that determine your condition of poverty or wealth.

As you can see, people do not fail to pay their bills for lack of money; they fail to honor their financial obligations for

lack of understanding of themselves and their relationship with money, as debts are paid in the first place by desire, conscience, discipline, emotional balance, a sense of responsibility and integrity. The transfer of money from one account to another is just a physical demonstration of the independence and financial maturity of each one.

# Abandon old concepts

If your intention is really to become a millionaire, in addition to clearing financial issues, you will need to abandon some false concepts of the past and overcome some traumas and complexes stored in your subconscious since childhood and youth regarding money.

It will be necessary to overcome emotional barriers, be they real or imaginary, because we do not see the world as it is, but as we are. This means that each human being lives conditioned by mental patterns, concepts and images created and fed by him about himself and the world around him.

We can say that each individual potentially has both misery and an inexhaustible source of wealth within him. It will grow, expand and manifest whichever is most intensely stimulated. In short, the belief you hold in your mind will prevail.

For this reason, believing in yourself, your ability to change your financial condition and your great potential for achievement is the basis for attracting unlimited wealth to yourself. It is by cultivating your inner millionaire spirit that you will discover new strengths to achieve what you aim for.

In a way, you are in this earthly existence to enable divine purposes to manifest through you, both for your own sake and for the sake of humanity. So, for all of this to happen, the first step is to believe in yourself. Imagine, as a mental exercise, that you and I are talking, sitting in a beautiful room, with all the comfort and convenience. The question I ask you is, "Do you believe in yourself? Do you believe you will get rich? Do you believe that you will have great possessions, that you will build fame and fortune and that you will be a millionaire, or perhaps a multimillionaire? ".

Throughout your life, you have probably answered negatively to all or most of these questions.

The more you can answer affirmatively to all of these questions, the more strength you will have to propel you towards your purpose. But I say that the more you can answer these questions positively, the more strength you will have to propel you towards your purpose.

## Test your perseverance

When you set out to start a transformation process, an interesting thing happens. It is as if there are forces that "pull" you back to your usual, already familiar and stable state, as this is a known path, even though it is no longer desired. Therefore, one thing I can guarantee: in your pursuit of prosperity, your desire, your discipline and your perseverance will be tested. It always happens and it happened to me too.

A few months after I started my modest enterprise, I found myself in an extremely precarious financial situation, in which I was content when the income was sufficient to cover the expenses of the month. Then, an "opportunity" arose for me to earn more.

An acquaintance of mine told me that the consulting firm Case Consultors, where he worked, was looking for a professional with technical training and commercial experience similar to the ones I had. According to him, the vacancy was practically mine, all I had to do was present for the interview.

The salary offered was wonderful, especially when compared to the ridiculous amount I took home at the end of the month. After reflecting on the proposal, I concluded that accepting the job offer would imply the cancellation of all my personal projects. So I called my friend, thanked him for the contact and informed him that I would decline the invitation.

Unhappy, he took the matter to his director and together they decided to schedule an interview with me to better explain the proposal. I refused the invitation a second time but, because of his insistence and as a courtesy, I decided to accept the interview.

I was received by Thomas Case himself, president of the company, who was accompanied by his vice president. The contact was brief, but I will never forget the sequence of questions and answers that took place at that meeting. After hearing a brief presentation of my projects, plans, strategies, goals and objectives, Mr. Case asked me: "Do you think you will make money from these English classes?". "Yes," I replied. And he continued: "Do you think you will be rich with these classes?" I replied: "I believe so". "Do you think you will make a fortune with your plans?" I said, "Honestly, I believe so." Then he asked one more question: "Do you have any reason to doubt the success of your plans?" I said, "No, sir."

As the interview was conducted in English, he looked at his colleague and exclaimed:

"This man is unhireable!" (this man is "unemployable").

Then we said goodbye and each one went his own way: him after his professional, and me after my dreams. That day, I knew there would be no return. It would be winning or winning.

When you are after your projects, make sure you are prepared for these moments of testing and setting the course, as this will happen to you. It is these "tests" that will help you to be sure of what you want, to better define your goal.Start at the right time

As I said, if you want to have a peaceful financial life, keep working as normal. However, if your plan is to get rich, millionaire or multimillionaire, sooner or later, you will need to start putting your life project into practice.

However, do not be in a hurry, as every individual who nurtures the millionaire spirit has its own pace of development and has a particular stage of preparation and qualification, regardless of age.

Some, already in their teens, acquire sufficient maturity to generate great wealth and others need to go through several sad and bitter experiences until they mature financially. There are still those who only discover their millionaire potential after retiring. Unfortunately, some spend their entire lives without ever discovering their inner wealth.

When you start your personal project, it is important to differentiate an income generating activity from the opening of a company. Please note that when I started teaching English I didn't rush to start a company. I was engaged in a revenue-generating activity in my home, but I did not yet have an open business. It only happened later.

Only after you have tested and approved your venture will you know that the time has come to take a solo flight and assume all the burdens and obligations of maintaining your own business. Perhaps, as it happened to me, for some time you will need to maintain two simultaneous activities, as long as they are not conflicting and competing with each other.

## Start from where you are

When analyzing the profile of millionaires from all over the world, we find some similarities in their trajectory. It is motivating to know that 90% of them started from scratch. In general, they were very poor people in the past and started their projects with few resources and a bag full of plans and goals. In the beginning, they almost always walked in solitude. They faced many challenges, rejections and criticisms. They walked blindly, not quite sure where to go, who to talk to or where to look for answers. However, they went on, in a tireless marathon of mistakes and successes until they managed to catch a glimpse of the light at the end of the tunnel.

So, rejoice, because according to this model you can also prosper. By zeroing in on your past, you are ready to start exactly where you are and get where you want to be. Throughout this journey you will need to strengthen your entrepreneurial spirit, without wasting your mental capacity by worrying about minor misfortunes, setbacks and setbacks.

To undertake, one must have a mind focused on the positive and the solutions. Your creative thinking needs to be focused on your greatest desires: houses, land, properties, automobiles, comfort, safety, health, education, leisure, recreation, travel, tours, clothes, good food, good bed and all that wealth can provide .

To undertake, you need to develop a trademark in the soul that is called initiative. People with initiative radiate optimism and confidence wherever they go. They do not wait for orders, but act on their own, because they cannot see the world happening around them without making their contribution.

The entrepreneur wants to achieve what has never been achieved and is not content with the harsh and sad reality of the moment, nor does he allow himself to be overwhelmed by adversity or accidents on the way. This vision takes you ahead of your time.

Entrepreneurial people believe in themselves and, even recognizing their limitations, highlight their strengths as much as possible. Although they have deep convictions, they know how to respect the opinions of colleagues and try to maintain a good relationship with everyone.

They are endowed with great power of concentration, their objectives and goals are well defined, tempered with a good dose of ambition. Per

in the end, they are extremely disciplined when it comes to acting, as they feel immense pleasure in doing what they do.

However, someone may ask: "What do I do if I have an entrepreneurial spirit, but right now I am in debt?". I have discovered, over the years, that the entrepreneurial ability to generate large sums of money and the competence to manage and multiply one's own resources are two distinct and separate sciences.

We rarely find talented people who are able to master these two techniques from an early age. We often find great entrepreneurs, but with disabilities in dealing with their own finances. So, if you've ever found yourself in a financially disastrous situation, don't be discouraged. You are a normal human being. I also went through this and needed support to overcome this inability. There is no dishonor in the fact that the person finds himself in difficulties, facing setbacks and financial setbacks.

No matter how unfavorable your current condition is, never accept it as permanent. The best thing to do is to become aware that something needs to change in the way you manage your money. First analyze, as I said earlier, what is the source of your debts, and then commit to adopting a healthier and more rational model in managing your own finances. I will talk more about that later.

People often ask me: how do you get so much motivation to carry out your projects? I will tell you a secret. While I was still at university, I started to form a personal library with motivational books on human relationships, leadership techniques and finance. These books gave me direction and filled the void of a hungry soul in search of self-reliance. Some of these books I even read several times.

I came to read over a hundred books to understand some essential principles of how to motivate myself in the pursuit of personal and

financial. They were works that contained simple, yet fundamental techniques, on how to set goals and achieve them, how to deal with adversity, how to overcome limits and, finally, how to build a life of growing prosperity.

This immersion in the fascinating world of positive literature has taught me that in order to increase my income I must first grow, as my habits of dealing with money will determine the size of my bank account.

As Napoleon Hill taught: "Each adversity brings with it the seeds of an even greater achievement". This means that everything you have learned, experienced and experienced up to this point was just a preparation for the achievements that lie ahead.

The laws of success, fortunately, are universal and do not discriminate against color, ethnicity, religion, culture or any physical or social condition. The laws of success are eternal, infallible and immutable. They were just as valid for the ancient pharaohs of Egypt as they served in this generation to form tycoons like Bill Gates, Steven Jobs, Sam Walton and so many other millionaires around the world. They also apply to you, your neighbor, your boss, an industrialist, an artist, a dentist, a teacher, an unemployed person, an executive, and even the individual who is currently in debt .

If you are really committed to becoming a millionaire, your biggest challenge will be to believe in yourself and your ability to do simple things to overcome all the pending issues of the past. In this way, you will be able to start a new life towards prosperity. So I recommend that you read this book several times. You will notice that with each new reading you will assimilate new concepts and feel closer to your millionaire destiny.

**To awaken the millionaire in you, remember:**

If you have debts, clear your debts first.

Do not be trapped by false beliefs of the past. •

Whoever understands interest receives, whoever does not understand pays.

First have an income-generating activity and only then start a business.

**Mentalize:**

I believe in myself.

My mind is focused on prosperity.

My trademark is called initiative.

I have an inexhaustible source of wealth within                                    me.

# Chapter 5

## Gold Key 2

## DaydreamUse your ability to dream

I discovered that all millionaires have something in common in their nature: the ability to dream. These entrepreneurs live almost as if they were hypnotized by their own dreams. They dream of scenarios that have not yet been created, with paths that have not yet been taken and products and services that have not yet been launched by the market. These dream-makers learned to think big and start small.

I really like this description by César Souza, consultant, author and speaker: "Dream-makers are ahead of their time. They have a sense of freedom to choose their path and a mixture of boldness and courage. They are not afraid to take risks, they do not accept no. Go and do what once seemed impossible. Despite the dynamism of running several projects at the same time, dream makers do not lose focus, do not waste time or energy on tasks that are not part of the dream ".

Millionaire entrepreneurs have learned to daydream. This means dreaming with your feet on the ground and having a constant awareness of personal renewal, without fear of abandoning old mental models rooted in your subconscious over the years and replacing them with a new emotional and spiritual dimension, almost always ignored by the majority.

This is a process that must begin with you and for you. When you dream of something or a personal transformation, you need to involve your mind, heart and spirit. That's why a burning dream is the most powerful tool you can have to achieve success. It is not just a vague and vague longing. To have a chance to come true, your dream needs to become an obsession with which you sleep, wake up and live 24 hours a day.

James Allen, author of the work As a man thinketh, stated:

Dreamers are the saviors of the world. As the invisible world keeps the world visible, man, through all his experiences, is also fed by beautiful visions of lonely dreamers. Humanity cannot forget its dreamers; he cannot let his ideals wither and die; these make it survive; it has them as the realities that it will one day see and know. Composers, sculptors, painters, poets, prophets and sages are the builders of the other world, the architects of heaven. The world is beautiful because they exist. Without them, hardworking humanity would die.

# Define exactly what you want

Sooner or later, you will need to define exactly what you want to achieve in the pursuit of prosperity. Perhaps you already have your own answers and are already moving in the right direction. If so, congratulations! You are on the safe path to reaching your first million. However, if you find yourself in a dilemma similar to the one I found myself in, without knowing which way to go, now it's time for you to ask yourself:

What is my dream?

What do I really want?

What do I want to do with my life?

Who do I want to be in society?

What legacy do I want to leave to the world?

As long as you do not stop and answer these questions very clearly, sincerely and honestly, you will remain like a boat adrift, thrown from a

side to side, according to the waves and winds of the moment. Without that definition, you will never reach a satisfactory destination.

If everything is created first in the mental dimension, then you will need to work with the mind so that it is your ally in the realization of your dreams.

For that, I suggest that you spend a weekend, a day or an afternoon with yourself. Choose a time that is free from interruptions and interference. Reserve quality time. You will need to relax, disconnect from the routine, analyze, reflect and meditate on your dreams and goals and on the new postures necessary to achieve them.

At that opportunity, give yourself a chance to review your values, ideals and goals. Give yourself time and analyze where you are going and where you want to go. Think deeply about who you really are and why you are here. Take the opportunity to consider all the possibilities on a personal, family, spiritual, professional and financial level.

In the same way that an architect mentalizes a project and then transfers it to paper, now you will transfer your dreams stored deep in your soul to the pa-pel. Do this through an exercise I call personal brainstorming.

# Do your personal brainstorming

Take a sheet of paper and a pen (or the computer, if you wish). Write down everything that comes to mind in the area of desires, goals, aspirations, ideals and dreams.

Just write, without questioning or trying to understand, explore or detail.

Allow your imagination to conceive your most daring dreams.

Be as comprehensive as possible in the list of aspirations, without sticking to any of them specifically.

Take your time. Use as much time as you need, as this is your moment.

Write whatever comes to mind, however daring your desires and thoughts may seem.

It doesn't matter if your ideals seem to be out of your reach at the moment. If so, that's why they are called dreams.

É    It is essential to consider everything that is hidden inside, even your most audacious dreams.

Don't worry about how your dreams will come true. History has shown that the universe itself provides ways to alter its course to meet the demands of those who, determinedly, seek to achieve their specific goals.

Now, having defined each goal, you will do a mental exercise that consists of mentalizing and repeating what you want to achieve. You will need to formulate a series of positive statements for each item. Do not make negative statements. For example, if your goal is to be prosperous, wealthy, millionaire, don't think of phrases like this:

I want to stop being poor.

I am tired of poverty.

I want to leave poverty behind.

If you think of a negative sentence about poverty, do you know what will happen? Poverty will increase! Your brain will attract, engrave and reinforce the image of poverty. Do you want to see proof of that? If I say, "Don't think about red," what color did you think of?

If you are initially unable to mentalize your statements, you can write them down. Then, repeat your phrases to yourself in the morning, afternoon and evening, indefinitely.

Do not worry about how they will take place. The gesture of specifying, writing and projecting an image is much more valuable than your skills

## Perceived current or past achievements.

Mentalize your positive affirmations until those desires are part of you, until you become an obsession and part of the fibers of your heart, mind and spirit. When you reach that point, prepare to witness wonderful events in your life.

You may question this concept, doubt it or criticize it. It does not matter. Do it anyway. Just as you don't quite understand how electricity works, you can be sure that if you put your finger in the socket it will take a shock. In the same way, you may not understand the powers of visualization, mentalization and repetition very well, but by doing this practice on a daily basis, you will soon be sure that these principles apply to you as well.

Try and see. The results will be surprising.

When you are mentally aligned with your biggest dreams, ask yourself:

Am I willing to sacrifice myself to make these dreams come true?

Am I willing to work 12, 14 or 16 hours a day in pursuit of those dreams?

Am I willing to do everything I can to achieve these goals? Am I willing to put aside certain pleasures, conveniences and comforts in order to pursue these ideals?

If your answers are positive for each of the questions above, congratulations! You are taking the first steps to awaken the millionaire in you. I am sure that you will be rewarded abundantly for your discipline.

Theodore Roosevelt said a phrase that I appreciate very much: "It is better to risk great things, to achieve triumph and glory, even exposing oneself to defeat, than to form a line with the poor in spirit, who do not enjoy much

nor do they suffer much, because they live in that gray gloom, which knows neither victory nor defeat ".

Explore your talent

You must consider your own talents in the pursuit of your dream. In general, we tend to imitate others, do what others do, sing the same song, paint the same picture. It seems to follow your own path quite difficult, but in order to have lasting success, you may need to leave the ranks of the crowd and march to the sound of the melody itself.

Think for a moment about the great directors of all time. Did they try to imitate someone? Did they want to repeat what had already been done? Did they all excel in the same area? No. Each one explored their own talent and many individuals stood out for doing something innovative and different from the models known at the time. However, do not put off putting your dream into reality by thinking only of something that has never existed before. You will have more chances of success in an enterprise whose objective is to improve an existing concept.

I found my success by teaching English. Note that teaching English is not an unprecedented concept, I did not invent this activity. This market has existed since the time when men decided to build the tower of Babel.

I often say that the secret to achieving success in any area is simple. You need to offer a product or service with high demand potential. The quality of your product or service needs to be superior to that of the competition. You need to deliver your product or service faster and better than the competition, and, finally, practice a fair price, which is not necessarily the cheapest price. Every consumer is willing to pay more for a product or service with these characteristics.

The success of the schools that make up the Multi Group is based on these four principles. We seek a concept of great demand (only 2% of the Brazilian population speaks a second language). We launched a quality education proposal with international certification (our students achieve international certification and achieve the highest score on the TOEIC exams®- Test of English for International Communication - in Latin America). We present satisfactory results faster than the competition (the student starts to speak English from the first class). And we have a fair price (our courses are accessible to a large part of the population).

## Establish your cycle of success

Whatever your dream or project, you need to imagine it and execute it within the cycle or wheel of success (see the figure on the next page). There are seven steps, some rational, some emotional, and some that bring these elements together.

First of all, every project starts with a simple idea, an objective to be achieved. At this stage, the idea is not ready, it is just a set of thoughts fragmented in your mind, similar to a puzzle with many pieces. As you exercise your creative power, it gradually gains shape, beauty and life.

Then, the idea evolves to the point of becoming a strategy that aims to achieve the proposed objective. In this phase, the target audience, the market potential, the characteristics of the sector, the distribution channel, marketing and customer service are considered.

# The cycle of succes

Then there is a very important step: turning these concepts, ideas and strategies into an action plan. This consists of transferring from the mind everything you imagined, visualized and conceived onto paper. In this phase, you define what you will do at each stage of the project, from start to finish.

By defining the strategy and an action plan, you are ready for the most important part: the action. There comes a time to stop all planning, organization and imagination and start implementing the plan. In this phase, many people get discouraged, give up and fail. Some are excellent planners, but poor performers.

When you execute your plan, you will discover something very interesting. Some plans work and others don't. Pessimists react like this: "The plan was so good, the prospects were so good, the market was so favorable! I don't know why it didn't work ". That's how the losers give up.

So, make sure that not all plans will always work every time. This situation takes us to the next step: assessment and course correction. Anyone who is committed to success will never take no for an answer.

Course correction, therefore, is a vital and ongoing element in any successful enterprise. At that moment, we change what needs to be changed and perpetuate the good practices already adopted.

Finally, it is time to celebrate the results achieved. At this point, it is important to recognize everyone who participated in the realization process until achieving the proposed objective so that they feel important, valued and participating in this achievement.

# Take care of your emotions and your reactions

As you strive to follow each step of the success cycle logically and rationally, you will need to work on your emotional side at the same time. This is perhaps the most challenging aspect of all, as it is related to your inner self, your thoughts and your belief system. I will describe this very important element of an emotional nature.

When visualizing your venture, it is important to understand the correlation between thoughts and obtaining favorable or negative results, because more important than what happens to you is how you react to what happens.

The same event can manifest itself in the lives of two people and each person will react in a different way: one may be irritated, exalted, rebel,To suffer, to suffer, while the other will be able to control, contain itself and transform itself.

What is the difference between the two? The way to interpret, process and organize your own thoughts, feelings and emotions. You may have noticed that poor people and rich people think very differently about money, people and the world around them. Your actions and reactions are governed by your way of thinking and, consequently, your state of peace or agitation, joy or sadness, love or hate, wealth or poverty, success or failure will be determined by the direct result of the commands that your brain sends to the body physicist.

The human structure, therefore, is a mirror and contains the exact expression of the way you organize, interpret and process your feelings, thoughts and everyday events. Unconsciously, you condition your brain to act and react in a certain way based on the impulses you receive and send to your mind at every moment.

Professor Trevisan, an international lecturer, teaches: "The conscious mind is the rational, objective mind; it is the mind that thinks, analyzes, reasons, deduces, draws conclusions, selects, censors, gives orders, determines, imagines; it is the mind served by the senses; it is the waking mind and responsible for what you are. The subconscious mind is the subjective, impersonal, non-selective mind, whose role is to carry out the orders it receives from the conscious mind through thought. Whatever the conscious mind accepts as true, the subconscious mind also accepts and accomplishes. The subconscious mind, which is linked to the spirit, has infinite strength, capable of fulfilling all your desires, but it never acts on its own; it acts in a very special way determined by thought ".

So, be specific in what you seek. The more specific you are, the greater your chance of hitting the target. Vague ideas and thoughts are not strong enough to generate the energy capable of transforming them into physical realization. A vague or generic goal, without a defined action plan, is just an illusion.

Remember that every materialized project came first in thought, in the mind of its creator. No matter the nature of the project, before it was carried out, someone had to conceive it, visualize it, imagine it. This is an eternal principle.

## Dreaming is living

When we lose the ability to dream, we lose the flavor for life.

There is a way to know if you are old: what is your mood when you get up in the morning? The young person wakes up with a strange sense of humor, a feeling that he may not be able to explain, but it is as if he says: 'This is my big day. This is the day when a wonderful thing will happen. ' The old individual, regardless of age, stands up with an indifferent spirit, without the expectation that anything important will happen. It will be just a day like any other. Maybe I hope it won't be any worse. Some people maintain the spirit of expectation at 70, others lose it early in life.

Remember that dreaming is good for the spirit, it inspires the soul, it helps you to feel its divine potential. Mark deeply in your heart that the desire to win is the secret of success, but the dream is the secret of desire.

So, from now on, start to meditate continuously on your dreams. Start to feel as if they have already materialized. Cultivate an unshakable faith with the certainty that your dream already belongs to you. The element of faith in the pursuit of your ideals is very important, because the more emotion and passion you put in your heart, in your heart, in your soul, the faster the materialization of your desires will happen.

Through your thoughts, your words, your feelings and your faith, you will be attracting the full realization of your highest and noblest ideals. So, dream with your mind on the stars and your feet on the ground.

**To awaken the millionaire in you, remember:**

Define exactly what you want to achieve.

The more specific you are, the greater your chance of success.

Do a personal brainstorming of your dreams and put on paper everything that is stored in the .

deep in your soul.

Visualize yourself already in possession of your desires and having already fulfilled your dreams.

Daily, feel the pleasure of conquest and victory in your heart.

Follow the success cycle of turning your goal into a strategy; create an action plan; execute, evaluate, correct the course, abandon what did not work, and perpetuate good practices and finally celebrate the good results achieved. Think big, start small.

•

**Mentalize:**

I dream big.

I think big.

I pay the price of success.

•

I believe in my drea

# Chapter 6

## Gold Key 3

### Desire to undertake to enrich Desire generates fortune

How many times have you heard that money makes money? I assert, vehemently, that money alone does not make money. Consider, for example, the financial investments of countries with stable economies: if we consider the inflation for the period and discount the Income Tax on the gain, we will soon conclude that the increase is minimal. There are also countless people who have inherited big fortunes or won a lot of money in the lottery and ended up losing everything after a few years for not knowing how to deal with the amount and multiply it.

Therefore, it is not just money that makes you a prosperous person. So, if money doesn't make money, how is it possible to be a prosperous person?

What will really make you a prosperous person will be your desire and your ability to undertake allied with reason and spirit well nourished with noble and lofty thoughts. This is the path to unlimited achievements and achievements. The deep, sincere and honest desire is the most valuable raw material you can have or develop to achieve your dreams.

Desire builds pyramids, bridges, highways, walls, stadiums, temples, discovers new lands, new planets, new stars, unveils mysteries of science, creates paintings and sculptures. Anyway, everything you contemplate around you is the materialized reflection of some individual's desire.

You may be asking yourself, but is entrepreneurship the only way to become a millionaire? No. There are scientists, doctors, lawyers, authors, high-level international executives who have reached this condition, but they represent less than 5% of new millionaires. The overwhelming majority win by the entrepreneurial spirit. It is important to note that 5% of these professionals who won in their sphere of activity were great entrepreneurs in their own area. Thus, the path to wealth necessarily passes through entrepreneurship, either in the business sphere or inserted in a broader context of leadership in an organization.

## Desire to win as you want the air you breathe

If you want to follow the path taken by more than 95% of new millionaires, I strongly recommend that you consider opening your own business. Begin to imagine, visualize and desire this condition. This desire must be vital, that is, it must be as strong as your need to breathe. The account below illustrates this principle very well:

On a beautiful sunny morning, in the middle of 400 BC, Socrates, the Greek philosopher, found himself meditating near a pond. Suddenly, a young man interrupted his concentration with the question: "What do I need to do to get wisdom?"

Faced with this universal question, the philosopher led him to the pond, dipped his head in the water and held it tightly. The young man managed to get rid of the force exerted by the philosopher and asked:

"What is happening? I just asked you a question

and you try to drown me! " The philosopher replied: "Do you want to get wisdom?" And the young man replied: "Yes, that is what I most desire". Again, Socrates sank the boy's head and, despite his resistance, held it tightly under the water for a few seconds. Desperate, the boy shouted: "What are you doing to me? I just want to know what to do to get wisdom! ".

And for the third time the Greek philosopher dipped the young man's head in the water.

The struggling young man, struggling, said: "Are you crazy? I came to look for you to know how to win in life and you try to take my life? ".

And Socrates replied, "When you desire wisdom as you desired air to breathe, then you will attain wisdom." That is why I say: when you want success as you want the air to breathe, then you will achieve success. To do this, your desire will need to become a constant obsession in your thinking.

# Find what you want

To get what you want, you will need to believe so much in what you want to accomplish to the point that you already have what you want and enjoy the benefits of this achievement.

For example, the entrepreneur who wants to open a school needs to imagine that he is already the owner of the most beautiful school in his city. He will need to view the well-lit facilities, the furnished and decorated classrooms, the spacious reception, the clean bathrooms, the modern multimedia laboratory, the large parking lot with the cars moving around, hundreds of students entering the school, attending classes , their graduation, the satisfaction on the students' faces and on their faces, their success and yours.

If you want, for example, to obtain the house of your dreams, try to imagine yourself already in possession of it. Feel like you are the owner of a spacious, spacious and beautiful home. Visualize the land, the facade, the rooms, the decoration, the chandeliers, the curtains, the furniture, the plants, the flowers, the trees, the garage, the swimming pool, the barbecue, the sauna, the sports court etc. See and try to feel, glimpse, visualize. Know that you will never achieve what you do not want with feeling, emotion and passion.

Dedicate all your energy to what you want to achieve. Confucius once said: "If a man does not think of what is distant, he will find what is around him sad". Speaking of dreams and achievements, Richard Devos, the dynamic founder of Amway Corporation, stated: "It is impossible to win a race unless you venture to run; it is impossible to achieve victory unless you dare to work. No life is more tragic than that of the individual who cherishes a dream, a ambition, always wishing and waiting, but never giving yourself a chance ".

Don't wait for the world to come to you. The respected American writer Keith DeGreen makes a beautiful point about this:

We all have a natural tendency to think that at any given time the whole world will knock on our door. The next time you find yourself dreaming about someone or something going to meet you, stop thinking and decide to do whatever is necessary to meet your great opportunity.

We need to resist the tendency to believe that the world will come to us, that things will happen for us. Instead, we are the ones who must go out to the world. If in fact the world ever walks to your door, it will only do so after discovering who you are and where you can be found. However, initially, you need to provide this information to the world.

You must make it clear and inform the world that you are here, that you have something valuable to offer and are eager to make it happen. Your talent can be huge, your potential can be excellent, but talent and potential not presented to the world will be worthless.

To succeed, you must get out of the crowd. So, from now on, decide to follow your deep instincts of entrepreneurship and achievement.

## The solution is in you

If you want to live in a better condition, there is no point in trying to fix your current situation from the outside in.

Instead of worrying so much about the outside world, you should be concerned about the inside world.

Remind yourself daily that you were born to progress and prosper. You were created with the full capacity to think, wish, dream, fight, undertake, accomplish, build, in short, win.

Now is the blessed day of your emancipation and financial independence. The time has come to awaken the millionaire in you. The joy, the happiness, the riches, all of this belongs to you and was created for you. These achievements are eagerly awaiting you to claim them. To do this, you will need sufficient humility to seek divine inspiration, which will supply you with all the answers you seek.

Finally, after taking a long walk in search of a dynamic, productive and prosperous life, you will discover that the path to the realization of your dreams begins in your heart. This seems to be the secret of the peace and serenity enjoyed by millions of people who have discovered the simple, peaceful and safe path to their true selves.

Therefore, decide right now to make any necessary effort to dive into the core of your being and, without any fear or prejudice, explore the potential installed there. Only then will you be able to reach full emotional, intellectual and spiritual stature to awaken the millionaire in you.

## To awaken the millionaire in you, remember:

Dedicate your time and energy to what you want to achieve.

Don't wait for the world to come to you; you need to reach out to the world.

See yourself in possession of what you most want to achieve.

Follow the path of entrepreneurship.

**Mentalize**:

I deserve to be a millionaire

I was born to progress and prosper.

I believe in my success.

•

I am a successful entrepreneur.

# Chapter 7

## Gold Key 4

### Determine how much you want to earn Determine your value

The money you receive today, for doing what you do, is exactly what you deserve to earn. There is no injustice in relation to your salary or remuneration, your boss, the company, wage policy, the government. You are the one who chooses to earn what you earn, because you chose to do what you do, where you do it and receive proportionately for it.

I am going to share here something that is not said in colleges and is not found in the best financial management books. In an invisible way, every individual carries a poster stamped with their own currency value. If we could read these posters, they would indicate: one minimum wage per month, five minimum wages per month, ten minimum wages per month.

The person who earns a minimum wage per month thinks that it is not worth more than that amount. Otherwise, I would make any necessary effort to earn more. The same is true for those who have an invisible sign that indicates five minimum wages per month. She sees herself as a person who is worth exactly five monthly minimum wages and nothing more. So much so that it is true that it has been receiving this amount for years and seems to be well accommodated and satisfied with its remuneration.

I know this is shocking, but it is important for you to think and analyze:

what value is stamped on your poster?

You get what you get for doing what you do. To illustrate this reality, I will use an example that I imagine is known to everyone: you know someone who has been challenged to qualify for a position of greater responsibility in the company. He was promised a salary increase as a result of the new performance. After several months, without observing any reaction on the part of the employee, the company ends up hiring someone from outside to fill the vacancy of higher remuneration.

Why does this happen? Because the person would even like to earn more, but, in the end, in his invisible poster he does not consider himself worthy or deserving a higher value or else he is not willing to do what is necessary to increase his own value.

In his false modesty, the person insists on increasing his curriculum with unfinished courses and projects. The company, in turn, cannot compensate for inertia or incompetence. Thus, by his own choice, the employee maintains the same position, the same salary, and ends up conquering a vulnerable position in the team.

There are still those who say: "I don't know what to do to improve my income". It is because in its invisible sign it says: "Here goes a person around the world who does not know what to do to increase his income".

Fortunately, this is not the case. You are already an educated and educated adult and no one needs to tell you what to do. I'm sure you don't even have to consult your boss to tell you how to become someone of greater value.

These answers are already within you. What is missing, in the first place, is that you change the value stamped on your invisible poster.

# A millionaire value

Have you ever wondered what value millionaires have written on their invisible poster? Those who have the millionaire spirit have the following indications on their poster: 1 million, 5 million, 10 million, and much more ...

However, they did not move to that level in a single leap. In the beginning, I had written much lower values, which gave them the self-confidence necessary to believe that in the future they could reach higher values. This also happened to me.

When I started teaching, I set an invisible value on my poster. At the time, all I wanted was to earn 10,000 reais a month. I imagined that, as a teacher, if I ever got that amount, I would be the most accomplished person in the world.

When I finally reached this level, I thought: if I change the value of my poster to 20 thousand reais, will this concept also work? Time has passed and the remuneration of the invisible value has materialized.

At this point, for the sake of experimentation, I thought: if the concept worked for 10 thousand reais and 20 thousand reais, we will soon change that value to 50 thousand reais to see what happens. After proving that the concept always worked, no matter what the value was on the poster, I no longer need to tell the end of the story. Grupo Multi's billing is now public information and has already surpassed billions of reais.

Most importantly, this concept is universal and works for anyone who trusts their potential millionaire. When you set a value for your poster, you commit yourself to delivering a similar value to people through your work, and it changes your professional life, as you need to qualify to be able to get that value.

I have already challenged hundreds of people to apply this concept and I was impressed by the number of people who came to me to say that they managed to transform their lives with him. Some have reported to me:"I changed the value on my invisible sign and it made all the difference in my financial life." "Thanks to the new value printed on my shirt, I have already reached my first million." "Now I know what it feels like to be a new millionaire."

I would like to affirm, with all certainty, that the same concept applies to you. Be certain that the simple fact of changing your inner value will already trigger a series of ideas and plans that will allow you, in a short time, to increase your earnings.

With a new value stamped on your chest, you'll be driven to try what you've never tried, to do what you've never done, to have what you've never had and to be what you've never been.

However, only you will be able to change your invisible value and, consequently, your remuneration. No one will do that for you, any manager, company or market. If you continue to do what you have always done, you will continue to get the results you have always obtained. If you want to get different results, you need to do different things.

## Increase your value

I will demonstrate here a practical exercise to help you increase your currency value. Take a sheet of paper or use the computer and describe everything you do professionally now and your current pay.

Set the new value you want on your poster
and write down what it is. Then, describe in
detail what you will do to receive what you
want to have and the date you want to reach
that amount.


**Date:**


**My current pay:**


**Full    description    of    what    I    do
professionally:**


**My new remuneration:**


**What will I do starting today to guarantee
my new remuneration: Date to achieve it:**

There is an inspiring thought, generally attributed to Ralph Waldo Emerson, on this theme: "The man who intends to win in life must subject himself to doing what needs to be done, even without having any taste,

trend or inclination for the task. By persisting in the execution of the task, you will eventually end up doing it well. Not that the nature of the task has changed, but the ability to do it has increased ".

## To awaken the millionaire in you, remember:

Change the value stamped on your invisible poster.

To have a different gain, you need to do different things.

**Mentalize:**

I'm millionaire.

I have the millionaire spirit.

I believe in my potential millionaire.

# Chapter 8

## Golden key 5

## Divide to multiply A successful model

When observing the victorious trajectory of the millionaires, we see that nobody has ever accomplished something great alone. All won by their ability to bring good professionals close to them and to form, train, motivate and reward a team committed to individual and collective success.

So it is a fact that the more you are able to help others succeed, the more success you will have. The more you join forces and share the glory, the more it will multiply. Whoever wants to win everything alone, who wants everything for himself, ends up with nothing in the end, because people don't like being around petty or selfish people.

To form your millionaire venture, consider the benefit you will make to countless people, and that will be the proportion of your success.

It worked for me. Twice a year, I hold the seminar "How to wake up the millionaire in you". This is one of my great satisfactions: being able to follow the transformation process in the lives of hundreds of entrepreneurial people, who believed in themselves, in their success, in their dreams and, in a short time, reached the status of millionaires.

For some, this transformation process is gradual and slow, but for others it occurs so quickly that they are surprised themselves.

É        it is natural that everyone wants success, but few have a model of success to follow. Fortunately, my professional success has enabled me to set up the largest school of entrepreneurs in the country and, thanks to the franchise model, which I adopted since the beginning, I have helped to train more than one hundred new millionaires in the last five years in Brazil.

Most importantly, most of them started from scratch. Each entered the franchise network with a different professional and academic background, but all with the following characteristics in common: a passion for teaching, a strong entrepreneurial spirit and a commitment to education as a life project.

## Transform your individual dream into a collective dream

The successful entrepreneurs did so thanks to their ability to transform their individual dream into a collective dream. When you believe enough in yourself, in your potential multiplier, you are ready to take an important step: to influence the people around you to embrace your dream.

When the people around you join you in pursuit of your dream, your enterprise will turn into something much bigger than yourself. The question that must be circling your mind right now is, "How do I make this happen?"

Before answering, allow me to ponder: Have you noticed how unsuccessful people are suspicious and always on the back foot? They do not believe in others and think that someone will harm them and outmaneuver them. They think that others are always up to something to get something out of them.

Sometimes, in a social circle, I come across people like that, full of fear and distrust. They often ask, "With so many schools in so many countries, aren't you afraid that someone will pass you by?"

I tend to reply like this: "I should have thought about it 25 years ago, when I started teaching, but not now".

Every entrepreneur who has the millionaire spirit trusts people. The owners of the largest companies always give a vote of confidence to those who work together with them, as they know that the best way to expand their business and multiply their entrepreneurial capacity (and their earnings) is to build a team with professional talents, which they receive precisely for their they do and as much as they collaborate.

# Build your talent team

On your entrepreneurial path to awaken the millionaire in you, you will need to form your talent team.

Next, I will show you the seven vital principles for success in building a winning team.

# The seven principles of winning teams

**Believe:** The first step in creating a winning team is to believe in people and their ability to achieve. To believe is to trust, and trust

é a value for those who give it and for those who receive it, because it creates a bond capable of giving solidity to any team.

**Train:** By truly believing in your team, you will dedicate time and resources to qualify, qualify and train your professionals. Well-trained teams produce four times more than untrained teams. Developing talent is one of the most rewarding challenges for a successful leader.

**Motivate**: As the leader of an organization, you will need to be the primary motivator for those who will be under your management. Your followers will be a direct reflection of you. If you are crestfallen, dejected, moody, your followers will do the same. If you have energy and enthusiasm, it will infect everyone. People are more motivated by appreciation, recognition and the opportunity for professional growth than just remuneration. Therefore, in order to retain talents in your team, it is essential to remember the emotional aspects.

**To delegate:** Whoever has the millionaire spirit needs to become familiar with the principle of delegation. Millionaires and successful professionals know that their time and capacity are limited and that is why they rely on the talent and experience of their team members.

**Go along:** Unaccompanied delegation and a combined deadline for the delivery of tasks is pure deception, both for those who give the order and for those who receive. Do not confuse delegation with "delegation". Whoever leaves the team loose, without monitoring and collection, may never hear about the delegated matter again.

**To assess:** Another important aspect for those who have a team is, from time to time, to bring the team together to evaluate results, establish priorities and correct the course. Often, the order of the cubes is questioned, when the need for the cubes should be questioned.

**Celebrate:** Always take the time to celebrate the results achieved. You do not need to rent a ballroom, hire a band and offer a banquet for each celebration. Different achievements require different festivities. Twenty years ago, when we started selling the first franchises, each time we closed a contract, we gathered the team and celebrated the achievement with pastries and guarana. The important thing is the spirit of respect, appreciation and gratitude to the team.Create a promising environment

I learned as an entrepreneur that the company does not dismiss or promote anyone. It is the individual who becomes unfeasible or promoted every day. As time goes by, he just waits for the moment of his dismissal or promotion to be formalized.

Therefore, the main role of the successful leader is to create a healthy and promising business environment. As a constant mentor, he must be tireless in his mission to train, train, motivate, accompany and finally celebrate the achievements with the team. There is an inspiring story for all leaders who have this mission:

There was a boy with little professional qualification who was looking for a job, and the only job he found was as an insurance salesman. He had never sold anything before, but he still accepted the job. After receiving the initial training, he went out on the street in search of customers.

In the first week, it didn't sell anything. In the second week, he sold insurance. In the third week, he sold nothing, and in the following week, he only made one sale. Result: his salary at the end of the month was small. The situation was repeated in the second and third months.

Unmotivated with his commission-based compensation, he went to his manager and resigned. The manager told him not to give up and invited him to attend a lecture to be given by the company's president, at the national convention, the following weekend.

Quite discouraged and already determined to quit his job, he accepted the invitation just so as not to offend the boss. On the scheduled day, he attended the event. The auditorium was packed with sales representatives, and the boy felt a little embarrassed and embarrassed in the midst of so many experienced people.

The president took the stage, was applauded and began his speech by saying: "I would like to congratulate you all for being excellent sales professionals". The poor guy thought, "Wow, he doesn't know me." The president continued: "Now I will prove to you how great you really are". The boy thought: "This one I want to see".

Then the president said the following: "We have about a thousand people in this auditorium. Is there anyone here who has never made a sale? If so, please stand. " There was general silence in the audience, everyone looked around, but no one stood.

And the president continued: "As you can see, everyone is an excellent salesman.

However, perhaps you are thinking: why do some sell more and others sell less? ". O

boy said to himself: "Wow, he read my mind. This is what I wanted to know ".

The president then replied: "Statistics indicate that we contacted an average of fifteen people to then close a sale. Each has a different sales history. Some sell more and others sell less ". The boy thought: "I must be the flashlight for these people". The presidenthe continued: "This means that when you go out to sell, you should expect to receive 15 'no' before you get 'yes', because 'no' is part of 'yes'".

"Wow, I never thought of that! The 'no' is part of the 'yes' ", he thought.

The president added: "So from now on, when you go out into the street to sell insurance, I want you to be happy to hear 'no', as you know that every time you hear a 'no' closer to 'yes' 'you will be. I will ask one more thing: that you write down daily how many contacts you made and how many 'no' it took until the 'yes' time came. You will notice that, over time, your skill will improve and you will not have to wait 15 'no' until you find the 'yes' ".

The president continued: "The reason why some sell little is because they leave early in the morning and hear two 'no's' and then say to themselves, 'Today is not a good day for sales'. In the afternoon, they hear two more 'noes' and come home frustrated. When the wife asks how her day went, they reply: 'It was terrible. Nobody wanted to buy anything today. ' Then, the next day, the same scene is repeated and so on, day after day, until contact number fifteen arrives. Then the sale finally happens. Furthermore, the inexperienced salesperson thinks that after closing a sale, immediately the next contact he will make will give him a 'yes', but that doesn't happen, he will need to climb the entire ladder again. Now I ask a question: who controls the 'yes' is the customer or the seller? ".

Most replied that it was the customer, some were confused, but the thoughtful boy replied to himself: the salesman. Yes that's right. The seller controls the 'yes', because the sooner he anticipates the greater number of 'no', the sooner he will find the 'yes'.

The lecture was over and the boy returned home with his hopes renewed. He did not ask for the bill, but decided to remain in his position and test everything the president said.

Result: in the following month he beat all sales targets and later he was the regional sales champion. After a year, he participated again in the national convention, but that time he took the stage to be awarded the national sales champion award.

When I think about this experience, the words of the American philosopher William James come to mind: "Compared to what we should be, we are only partially awake. Our instincts are restrained, our plans are controlled, we only use a small part of our physical and mental resources ".

## Always be a seller

The salesperson's story also reveals an aspect that I consider fundamental: it doesn't matter your education or profession, it doesn't matter if you are a teacher, programmer, accountant, salesperson, actor or professional. You will never be a millionaire if you are not a salesman.

I have found in practice that successful professionals are focused on performing specific tasks, but millionaires are focused on selling. You are probably thinking, like the young man in the story, "But I'm not a salesman" or "I don't know how to sell anything" or "I never sold anything!". However, I say that if you really want to be a millionaire, you will need to develop this qualification, just like that young person developed, to always sell: your name, your image, your talents, your skills, your experience, your skills, your gifts and your results you can deliver as a professional.

You can be the best professional or the most talented person there is; if you are unable to sell your services or products, the world will never benefit from them and you will not be rewarded for it, and consequently you will never be able to get your first million. Take note of this: millionaires love to sell.

There is nothing more rewarding than the success you help to create. As long as I live, I will be very pleased to remember a brief conversation I had with a franchisee at a convention. It was after midnight, the band was still playing in the main hall, and my wife and I were heading for the bedroom when we were interrupted by a young franchisee. He said: "Today I consider myself a super-fulfilled person and I would like to thank you for that, because this year I turned 30, my little girl was born, I bought my house, I paid for the house more than one million reais, in cash, and the car in the garage is a BMW ". At that moment, we were thrilled with his success, we embraced and celebrated together the victories of that young entrepreneur.

Recently, I was very honored with another example of entrepreneurship. One of Grupo Multi's franchisees entered the Guinness Book of Records as the youngest entrepreneur in Brazil. He reached his first million reais before turning 21 and, since then, he has been interviewed by several newspapers, magazines and TV stations to share his fantastic story of overcoming.

When we help others get what they want, they help us get what we want most.

**To awaken the millionaire in you, remember:**

Transform your dream into a collective dream.

Help other people achieve success.

Form a team of professional talents.

Millionaires love to sell.

**Mentalize:**

I believe in people.

I invest in forming my team.

I qualify my team.

I delegate tasks and responsibilities.

I accompany my team.

•

I celebrate with the team the results achieved.

# Chapter 9

## Gold Key 6

## Save every penny to collect your million

## Saving is more important than winning

There is a link that links desire and financial prosperity, and I will tell you what it is. If you want to truly prosper, you will need to learn to save, accumulate and multiply any and all money you receive and will receive from now on.

Mark well: part of your income does not belong to you. Part of what you earn belongs to the formation of your assets and personal wealth. Know that if you are not concerned with forming your wealth and wealth, no one will do it for you.

If we ask a hundred people on the street if they save, save, save part of their salary every month, I can guarantee that of the hundred people only two or three will answer "yes". That is why there is so much poverty in the world and so few are able to abandon poverty and move on to wealth.

"But I earn so little, how am I going to save?", Is the most common question. I'm sure we all know people who earn a minimum wage and arrive at the end of the month with some money in their pockets. On the other hand, we also know people who they earn ten minimum wages per month and when the end of the month comes, they have a negative account, with their overdraft overdue, their credit card overdue, and they will have already loaned a buck from their father-in-law or brother-in-law, or even have already pawned his jewelry at Caixa Econômica Federal, or resorted to borrowing money from loan sharks.

This is because these people have not yet learned how to make a budget, financial planning, they have not learned to differentiate needs from desires, and they also do not have any methodology for dealing with their own money.

Without the practice of these concepts vital to the generation of prosperity, they are hostage to their own financial inability and thus are easily dominated by their consumerist impulses. They can even earn a lot of money, but without being programmed to manage it, they end up with nothing, so they never get rich.

So, if you want to become a millionaire, focus on earning, saving and multiplying your money. If you prefer to remain poor, spend everything you receive.

## How to multiply your wealth

If you have ever felt depressed, frustrated or defeated by your inability to manage your money, don't despair. I also had the experience of feeling completely illiterate in the financial area. I discovered that there is a big difference between knowing how to win and having the competence to conserve and accumulate wealth.

I had to learn this lesson with great difficulty and I had to change my old habits and concepts to deal with my finances until I could reach a state of unlimited prosperity. If I managed to change my financial condition, you can also achieve this result by following the same formula that I followed. I'll tell you how it happened.

When the Wizard network completed ten years of existence, we already had 200 schools throughout Brazil. So, we decided to make a convention in Orlando, Florida, to celebrate that moment in style. We elaborate an intense program, with activities, tours, dinners, awards, workshops and lectures. Anyway, it was an unforgettable event.

One night, away from the crowd and the glamor of that wonderful event, sitting in the solitude of my room, my wife Vânia interrupted my private celebration with the following question: "I don't know why you are so happy, so excited and so excited". I replied: "My love, we have many reasons to celebrate. After all, ten years ago I was unemployed, I didn't know what I would do in the future, I had no professional prospects. Now we have a great school with thousands of students all over Brazil, we generate thousands of jobs and we contribute to the education of our country ".

So she challenged me with this question: "Do you know how much we have in our bank account?" "Honestly, I don't know," I replied. At that moment, she ended my party with this answer: "Know that after ten years of commitment, dedication, sacrifices and hard work, all we have managed to accumulate in our bank account is 3 thousand reais".

From that moment on, that number no longer came out of my head: 3 thousand reais! I kept thinking: "Three thousand reais after ten years of work. All the work of ten years to finally get 3 thousand reais. Is someone financially successful with 3 thousand reais? ".

A few months later, I read an article in an in-flight magazine, which would change my financial condition forever. He dealt with different financial management models in a company. The author explained that generally large companies do, in the second half of each year, a long budget preparation exercise for the following year. After many meetings, negotiations and adjustments, the budget is finally approved

by the board, the presidency, the board of directors and the shareholders. In this way, all executives, managers and their teams start the new year committed to the eternal process and juggling to stay within the budget. After twelve months, the financial results are presented, evaluated, celebrated by some and regretted by others.

According to the author of the article, that model applied very well to large corporations, to publicly traded international conglomerates and to their published balance sheets. However, the article presented a new, revolutionary and challenging concept in the way of managing the finances of small and medium-sized companies. The concept is so simple that it comes down to three words: saving at the source.

The moment I read those words it seemed that the letters were jumping off the page and that they were written directly to me. At that moment, I clicked on my head and woke up to a new reality, as I had worked for ten years and all I had managed to accumulate was 3 thousand reais. That reading made me change my whole way of dealing with my finances.

## Saving at source

The concept of saving at the source applies both to those who have their own business and to those who have a salary or other forms of income. This way of managing your finances consists of predetermining, pre-defining, prefixing in advance what profit margin you want to obtain from your business or your income.

For example, if you define that you want 20% of profit, when receiving each part of your salary or each time a new resource passes through your hands, you will immediately separate 20% of your income to an account destined to the formation of your patrimony.

However, you must be wanting to ask me: "But, if I withdraw 20% of my earnings, how will I spend the month? How will I pay the bills? How will my expenses be? ".

Again, the concept is revolutionary. You separate what you are going to save and live with the rest, no matter what your salary or income. You literally ignore 20% of your earnings and survive on 80%.

When I understood this concept, I realized that if I kept the same pattern of spending everything I received, no matter how much my income increased, another ten years would pass and I might continue with my 3 thousand reais.

If I really wanted to change my financial condition, I would need to radically change the way I deal with money. And that is what I did, both personally and in my companies.

Thanks to my wife's severe warning that night in Orlando, and the decision, discipline and persistence in applying the concept of "saving at origin", over the years that followed Wizard stepped out of the reality of 200 schools to become one of the largest educational and business groups in Brazil.

We would never have reached the levels of achievement that we had had it not been for this valuable principle. And certainly until today, with each new revenue we receive, we separate the percentage reserved for the equity formation account.

Right now, I suggest that you interrupt your reading and do a mental exercise. Analyze your current financial situation, whether your income comes from your salary, your business or other sources. If your intention is to awaken the millionaire in you, define exactly what percentage will be allocated to the formation of your millionaire account.

Define today how much you will save each time new money passes through your hands, no matter how much you earn or how long it will take for your fortune to accumulate. More important than the

the value or the time it will take will be your commitment to the application of this valuable principle, because, with it, your assets will inevitably increase.

To get rich it is not enough to save, you will also need to increase your ability to generate new income. However, by using this method continuously, you will start to accumulate the great wealth that will be part of your life from now on.

# Unlimited wealth

It is known that 1% of the planet's population earns 96% of all income produced on Earth. Does this happen by luck, by chance, by accident or by some financial strategy? The answer is simple: people with a millionaire spirit have learned to apply the principles of how to turn their income into fortunes.

To accumulate 1 million reais, you must first accumulate 100 thousand reais. To accumulate 100 thousand reais, you must first accumulate 10 thousand reais. To accumulate 10 thousand reais you must first accumulate 1,000 reais.

If you do not follow this model, you will never be a millionaire! All who won and made a fortune underwent a financial methodology, applied with a high degree of discipline and self-control. They learned that more important than killing yourself is to create a condition where money works for you. They also discovered that it is never too late to start applying these rules in their daily lives.

Note the words of anthropologist George O'Neil about the process of personal change:

Changing is never that simple. What is really implied is not the liberation of the authentic self, but the formation of a new self, a self that gradually transcends the limitations and smallness of the old. This can only be done by doing it differently when interacting with other people. New strategies will have to be developed, expressing new intentions and encouraging others to take part in better human relationships.

Believe in your capacity for personal and financial transformation. Know that in the depths of your being there is an unlimited potential for achievement. You have within you the divine power to be, do and have anything you want.

**To awaken the millionaire in you, remember:**

Define the percentage that you will separate when receiving any money that reaches your hands.

Disregard the total value of your income and live only with what will not be destined to form your future assets.

Before receiving your remuneration, make a detailed budget defining the destination of your resources.

**Mentalize:**

- I form my personal wealth.

- I form my personal assets.

- I have a millionaire account.

- 

My millionaire account grows every day.

# Chapter 10

## Golden key 7

## Believe in your divine origin

T every successful person carries with them the feeling of being fulfilling a mission, because any victory loses its value if we do not use it for even greater purposes. It is difficult for someone to feel totally fulfilled without experiencing the feeling of being connected, in some way, to the higher purposes of life. Thus, everyone who wishes to feel

the full aroma of success will need to feel in harmony with the Creator.

A channel of communication with the divine

From a young age, I learned from my own experience that when a person establishes a channel of communication with his divine origin, he acquires more strength to persevere in the pursuit of his dreams. She can more easily identify her gifts, her talents and her skills, increase her self-control and be able to focus on her potentials and priorities. He also learns to deal with daily oppositions in a positive way, as he sees everything as a process of learning and maturing, and not as a permanent limitation.

My spiritual formation was given by my parents. When I was 12, they sought answers to the soul's questions: What is the origin of humanity? What is the purpose of life? Where do we go after death? How to reconcile work and family life? How to maintain

united family? In that moment of reflection, with seven young children to raise, they got to know the Church of Jesus Christ of

Latter-day Saints, whose Christian teachings showed them a safe path towards

à personal, temporal and spiritual fulfillment, and passed these concepts on to the family.

James E. Faust wrote words inspired by his book How to find light in a dark world that shows the importance of the spiritual dimension for everyone:

Spiritual peace is not found in race, culture or nationality, but in our commitment to God. Each of us, regardless of our nationality, needs to dive into the innermost recesses of the soul to find the divine nature that is deeply ingrained in us and sincerely pray to the Lord to endow us with wisdom and inspiration. Only when we reach the bottom of our being will we discover our real identity, our own merit and our purpose in life. Only when we try to get rid of selfishness and worry about rewards and riches, will we find the sweet relief of anxieties, wounds, pains, sufferings and unrest in this world. God will not only help us to find sublime and eternal joy and satisfaction, but He will also change us.

Believing in our divine origin sustains and inspires us. In our daily lives, it manifests itself in our feelings, our impressions, our intuition, our inspiration and in an inner voice. Have you ever heard these whispers that come from the depths of your soul? Certainly, yes.

As you try to hear that inner voice, it becomes more and more perceptible to your senses. Suddenly, she starts talking to you more often, and you start to trust her more and more. It is not just about feeding your ego, but about discovering who you are, who you can become and how you can bless your life and the lives of those around you more immensely.

I really like Ella Wheeler Wilcox's thinking about the position of the human soul before the seas of life. Notice this beautiful comparison:

A boat sails east

and the other to the west.

Both are carried by the same wind.

It is the position of the candles,and not the wind

that gives us the direction.

Like the winds at sea, so is destiny;

and when we travel through life,

é   the position of the soul that decides which way,

neither calm nor rivalry.

The strength of the wind is powerful, however, the same wind can transport a boat on the right or on the left. The direction of the boat is not determined by the wind, but by the position of the sail. It is the same with the direction of your soul and your destiny. By positioning your life in a spiritual dimension, often ignored, you will begin to feel a deep inner peace that will fill the void of your soul and point you to a safer and more promising destination.

# Develop your spiritual dimension

I would like to suggest an experience that will help you in your contact with your spirituality. It is a personal gesture that will require an attitude of humility, meekness and reverence on your part.

This experience consists of the following: set aside time for meditation and reflection. Choose a place, day and time when you are free from interruptions or interference. If possible, stay in touch with nature, in front of the beauty of the mountains, the countryside or the sea. You will know how to choose the most appropriate place.

When you are in that reserved place, start talking, in a spirit of thanksgiving, with the Creator. You can start by thanking us for the creation of the world, for the warmth of the Sun, for the beauty of the Moon and the stars, for the air you breathe, for your conception, for your gestation, for your birth.

Give thanks for your body, your organs, your limbs, your mind, your intelligence. Give thanks for your first days of life, for your mother, for your father (even if he is unknown), for your childhood, for your family members, for their first years of life, for the first day of school, for their teachers, for their neighbors, for their childhood and youth friends.

The more complete and more detailed your thanks are, the more effect it will have. Continue with your spirit of gratitude through all phases of your life until you reach the present day. Take your time. You may choose to write down your feelings at this point. Follow the impressions of your heart, because the important thing is that you recognize the hand of God in each phase of your existence.

With that constant attitude in your heart, you will develop your spirituality more and more. You will create a spiritual connection or connection with the Creator and, with a spirit full of gratitude, you will be more prepared to be guided by God towards the fulfillment of your most sincere desires.

What a joy to know that you can maintain a link with the Creator Himself, a heavenly, omnipotent, omniscient being, source of all light, intelligence, wisdom and love! As a child of God, this universe belongs to him as a legitimate inheritance. The most important thing is that you are also heir to the divine characteristics, attributes and gifts.

Make sure you are not alone. God, as a loving Father, is always at your disposal. Try to speak to a mortal and you will have the greatest difficulty in making an appointment, scheduling a date, and still have to call ahead to confirm the meeting. Almighty God humbly puts himself at your disposal at any time of the day or night, and you can reach him wherever you are: at home, at work, at school, in the countryside, on the streets, in moments of joy or in pain.

Note Keith DeGreen's inspirational thinking about temporal blessings: "As long as money is the quality of the services we provide to others, accumulating it is noble.

As we use our money in the service of those we love, supplying them with all

the warmth, comfort and safety possible, the expenditure is rewarding and divine ".

It would actually be inconsistent to think that God, being Father of love, Creator of all wealth, of all fortunes, all ore, countless mines of diamonds, silver and gold, prevented his children from enjoying his creation. So, thank God for the wealth that exists around you and at your disposal.

## All that wealth is yours. It belongs to you.

However, I need you, as a legitimate heir, to claim these blessings from the hands of the one who created them. Remember those words: "Everything you ask the Father in faith, believing that you will receive, will be granted to you". This passage includes talents, abilities, gifts, love, marriage, children, land, houses, apartments, automobiles, companies, industries, that is, everything that your heart desires.

## A divine chain

I would like to share a personal feeling. I know that God is part of our life, He inspires, consoles, enlightens, guides, forgives, strengthens, prepares and qualifies. When I think of the success I achieved in my professional career, I have the feeling described by the apostle Paul: "I planted, Apollo watered, but it was God who provided the growth". I feel God's protective hand helping me to overcome each stage of my entrepreneurial ascension.

I really like what Dr. Marcus Bach says about the divine power in our lives:

There is a kind of divine chain ready to take us between certain stages of life, and the more we perceive it and give ourselves to it, the better off we are. However, only those who have the courage to believe in it, the audacity to wait for it, the wisdom to understand it and the prudence to agree with it will benefit from this divine strength.

I have no doubt that my educational endeavor was born under the influence of divine inspiration. I have a deep sense of gratitude to God for this precious gift that he has entrusted to me. I am aware of the professional, social and moral responsibility that rests with me, and knowing that I am not alone in this majestic undertaking gives me a lot of security, serenity and confidence to carry forward the dreams I once created.

**To awaken the millionaire in you, remember:**

Listen to your inner voice.

Cultivate your spirit of gratitude.

Recognize the hand of God at all stages of your life.

**Mentalize:**

- I am a son of God

- I have divine gifts and attributes.

- My life has direction and purpose.

  I can count on unconditional spiritual support at any time.

# Chapter 11

## The time has come for change

You are not yet aware, write to remember: change is the only constant in life. The universe is constantly changing. The world around us is constantly redesigning, discovering and innovating. The greater your ability to adapt to these changes, the greater your chance of triumph.

## Change is needed

People are very resistant to change, because they get used to doing the same things day after day, as if they were programmed like robots to act in a certain way. They end up settling for inferior results, forgetting that they can do more. There is a story that illustrates this very well:

There was a young man who spent his days wandering the banks of a river in search of precious stones. He was tireless in the search for stones of great value. He often walked for days, weeks and months and found only ordinary stones. When he found a gemstone, he put it in the bag. The worthless stones were thrown back into the river. It so happens that, after so long conditioned to throw ordinary stones back into the river, sometimes he found a precious stone and, by virtue of habit, without realizing it, he ended up throwing the precious stone back into the water.

Perhaps conditioned to old paradigms or mental patterns, until today you had missed chances and opportunities. However, the time has come for change! From now on, commit to moving forward, overcoming your limits and keep growing more and more!

Usually, people do not change when they feel good, but when they are down, depressed or frustrated. When we reach the point of unbearable non-conformity, the tendency is to do much more than we are doing. Suffering impels us to those moments of great decisions, after all, we are suffering. So, finally, we take action and change the course we are taking. Ralph Waldo Emerson, renowned American philosopher, declared:

Our energy stems from our weakness. Only after we are caught, stung and painfully hit, does aroused indignation armed with secret forces. A great man is always wishing to be small. While he is accommodated in the comfort of advantages, he sleeps. When he is pressured, tormented or defeated, he has the opportunity to learn something. Acquires wit and maturity. He gained facts, he learned about his ignorance, he is cured of the insanity of presumption. He acquired moderation and true skill.

I'm sure you don't want a life of suffering and deprivation. So, you are at the ideal point to change what it takes to live the life you always wanted.

## Chaos is part of the change

When you consciously start a process of change, know that you are taking care of the soul. In the beginning, you will have the feeling of uncertainty, insecurity, instability, because every change generates a stage of chaos, be it physical or emotional.

Think about the last time you decided to do a little renovation in your home. Perhaps the intention was just to change the look of the kitchen, but suddenly the sink changed, which no longer matched the taps, the cabinets, the floor and, finally, it was necessary to change the stove and even the refrigerator.

Often, a process of change ends up generating other changes that were not conceived in the beginning. Therefore, most projects end up taking twice as long as we imagine and, consequently, end up costing twice as much.

Imagine that subway project that will benefit the population and facilitate public transport, making it faster, cheaper and safer. Before the benefits can be enjoyed, there will be excavations, earth displacements, demolition of properties in its course, trees, parks and gardens will be sacrificed, not to mention the potential risk of accidents and the real chaos that the period will become during the works .

Think of the woman who wants a child. Imagine all the expectation, the anxiety and the preparation and the feeling of soon being able to embrace your little boy. Suddenly, pregnancy brings insomnia, discomfort, pain and unexpected complications, she will undergo several tests until the blessed day of the child's birth.

Perhaps that is why we have resisted change so much. We fear what will happen to us when we compare before, during and after. Another reason for resisting the changes is the fact that we are in a constant process of mental reconditioning. There seems to be a force, similar to the force of gravity, that binds us to old mental models. There is a story that describes this characteristic of human nature very well.

Once upon a time there was a newlywed young woman who wanted to please her husband, who liked steak with onions. Every morning, she would go to the butcher shop, buy a steak, then come home, split the steak in half, fry one half, fry the other half and serve the two halves to her husband.

She did this for three months. Without wanting to hurt his wife, one day the boy said: "Honey, you

é a great cook and a wonderful wife. I just wanted to know why every morning you go to the butcher shop, buy a steak, come home, cut the steak in half, fry one half, fry the other and then put the two halves on the plate? ".

The young woman's response was, "I learned from my mother."

One fine day, her mother-in-law appears in her house. The young husband takes advantage of the lady's presence and starts a conversation: "Dear mother-in-law, your daughter is wonderful and cooks very well, but there is something she does and I don't understand". He told the scene to his mother-in-law and asked for an explanation. The mother-in-law replied: "It was my mother who taught me this way".

Then, one fine day, the grandma appears in the house. The young man couldn't resist and asked: "Grandma dear, you have a wonderful granddaughter who cooks very well, but there is something she does and I don't understand". And he told the story to Grandma and asked him for an explanation.

"But there is an explanation, my grandson," said the lady. "A long time ago, when I got married, I got a frying pan as a wedding present, and it was very small. So I had to leave thesteak in half to fry it! ".

This story portrays the reality of many people who are stuck with old habits, customs and behaviors, without realizing how they originated and perpetuated themselves; they live conditioned by old mental models and find it difficult to adapt to new realities.

From decades to decades, society reorganizes itself: its basic visions, its social and political structure, the arts, its key institutions. Every fifty years, there is a new world. And people who are born at that time cannot even imagine the world in which their grandparents lived and where their parents were born.

How many people do you know who only attended high school and never started college? They think that they will be able to win professionally only with a secondary school level. They feel justified, because their parents had only a few years of study.

How many professionals do you know who are unable to use a computer productively? Many are competent, but rely more on their own memory than on the computer's memory. How many people do you know who, even though they have conditions, are not internet users? They are afraid of technological innovation. They feel intimidated and vulnerable in the face of such a powerful tool. They think that Facebook, Skype, iPod, iPad, in short iTudo, and so many others are concepts that will never dominate.

There are other hidden barriers, even more sensitive and profound, installed inside some people, which need to be overcome.

## Change consistently

There are people who say, "I have to take a 180-degree turn in my life." Congratulations! The objective, the intention and the purpose are correct. Don't expect, however, that suddenly, overnight, you will become the new individual you hope to be.

Awareness of the need for change slowly arises within us. Little by little, we feel overwhelmed with dissatisfaction, sometimes for no specific reason. However, deep down we know that something needs to change. Then there is a deep non-conformity with the existing situation, which impels us to action.

Note the words of Napoleon Hill, an expert in the techniques for achieving success:

A burning desire to be and to do is the starting point for the dreamer. Dreams are not born out of indifference, laziness or lack of ambition. Remember that almost everyone who has won in life has had to go through setbacks first and then enough trials to discourage them before they achieve their goal. The moments of decision in the lives of those who win tend to occur at the height of a crisis, during which they find themselves face to face with the other side of their personality.

Even though conscious, willing, determined and committed to change, the change is not immediate. We have a natural tendency towards immediacy, we want everything for today, here and now. However, any significant and lasting change requires time, patience, discipline and vigilance, until it is consolidated.

Have the humility to start from where you are and don't suffer thinking about where you should be. Francisco de Assis already taught: "Start doing what is necessary, then what is possible. And suddenly, you are doing the impossible. "

Old habits have been rooted for years in the depths of your being. They had a very strong power in their mental conditioning. That is why, sometimes involuntarily, you will find yourself practicing the same deviations, "addictions" and mental patterns that you have practiced for so long. Don't let yourself be overwhelmed. The solution is to break old ways of thinking and abandon old paradigms.

Errors and successes are part of the learning and transformation process. Remember that more important than speed is knowing that you are on the right track.

His process of personal transformation is comparable to the experience of climbing a ladder against a wall. You need to step up by step; however well-intentioned it may be, you cannot climb a whole staircase at once, unless you step on one step at a time.

Each step represents an advance, a new achievement, a new platform that supports the next step. If we try to skip a step, an accident can happen, we can injure ourselves, slow down or interrupt the growth process.

Another common trend is to think that something external needs to happen in order to make an inner change possible. Once, a very distressed and distressed colleague came to me. He had made some wrong choices and, consequently, faced a series of personal, financial and family difficulties. As we talked, he repeated several times: "Something has to happen in my life, something has to happen in my life".

I felt that he was saying this as if it had nothing to do with the adverse situation he faced, it was as if he were the victim of acts of others, as if he were involuntarily destined to suffer, perhaps because of some mysterious and hidden force. In fact, he lacked humility, sensitivity and wisdom to understand that the problem he suffered from was self-imposed. He himself had attracted and, as a result, created the adverse situation he faced.

Have you ever felt like that individual? Have you ever been waiting for something external to happen to cause an inner change? Maybe yes. However, if any change occurs, this transformation process will begin in your heart, pass through your heart, come to thought and manifest in your words and actions.

We cannot blame anyone for our current situation. If the blame is not on others, then is there something wrong with me, in my way of thinking, reasoning, feeling, acting and reacting to the events of each day?

## Ponder and answer:

**W**hat am I postponing to do and that if I did it would result in a huge difference in my life?

What prevents me from starting to act immediately?

Perhaps, if answered sincerely, these questions will become the greatest contribution you can make to yourself towards your happiness and personal well-being. Congratulations! The simple fact that you are reading this book demonstrates your high sensitivity, intelligence and initiative to make any necessary changes to awaken the millionaire in you.

**To awaken the millionaire in you, remember:**

Identify what you are putting off doing and what you do would result in a huge difference in your life.

Analyze what keeps you from starting to do these things right away.

Decide to make these changes, no matter what the cost.

**Mentalize:**

- I am an eternal apprentice.

- I am in an eternal process of transformation.

- Errors and successes are part of my progress.

The greater my capacity for change and adaptation, the greater my triumph.

# Chapter 12

## Thrive towards success

Pense for a moment: who has the greatest talent or the greatest chances of winning in life, the shipbuilder or the helmsman? An economist or a gardener? The dancer or the shoemaker who sews the sneaker? The peasant who plows, plants and nurtures the crop or the one who

reap?

Who has the most valuable skill: the shepherd, the shearer or the weaver? The violinist or the one who makes the violin? What extracts the stone from the mountain or the sculptor?

Before answering, read the following reports. They might as well contain your name. These are true stories, which did not happen in China or in the American Old West, but here, on Brazilian soil.

## An enterprising gardener

After the wedding ceremony and honeymoon trip, Norberto and Rosângela were at home talking about their future. They were very happy because they loved each other very much, but both had only one concern: Norberto was in debt and unemployed.

"And now, what to do?", They pondered.

In the following days, Norberto claims to have gone through a period of deep introspection and meditation, after which he felt an impulse, an inspiration, as if an inner voice said to him: "You can be a gardener". He pretended he didn't even hear that whisper. In his heart, he thought: "I always wanted to be an executive, work in an air-conditioned office, wear a white shirt and tie. Being a gardener? No way. Work under the sun, under the rain, keep your clothes and hands dirty with soil. What will my wife think? What will she say? ".

However, that little inner voice kept telling him: You can be a gardener. And, as he was unemployed and needed to support his family, he decided to believe his intuition andto venture as a gardener. He concluded that he would only need scissors and few tools to start working.

Even without experience, training or qualifications, and imbued only with the millionaire spirit, he started to clean the first gardens. In less than ninety days his schedule was packed with customers. After a few more months, he was already refusing service from people, who now came knocking on his door. At that moment,

Norberto claims to have had a second inspiration: "I can continue working alone or I can share this market with helpers, assistants and assistants".

So he decided to hire some helpers, and soon he had a team of gardeners working for him. After a few more months, Norberto realized that the "madams" spent more money on plants, flowers, trees, land and manure than on the service he provided. This was another turning point in his entrepreneurial career: "Abandoning gardens, abandoning helpers, just selling products to customers? Can I reconcile the two activities? ".

At that time, Norberto felt that he could significantly increase his income if he kept the customers and also supplied the plants. By this time, he was making enough money to buy a used Kombi, with which he made purchases and deliveries himself. After talking to his wife and enthusiastic about the flourishing of the business, he rented land and set up a small flower shop.

Rosângela took care of the counter, and he was in charge of the gardens, the helpers, the clientele and now the purchases and the direction of the new business.

Later, already quite convinced of the success of his enterprise and looking at the green and flowery horizon before him, he acquired the courage to transfer his activity to the prestigious neighborhood of Morumbi, in São Paulo.

Norberto Carlos Lopes became the owner of a successful gardening and landscaping company in the capital of São Paulo. He began to serve both homes and businesses. Throughout a thorny but very prosperous career, Norberto managed to accumulate a small fortune. With the resources saved, he built, rented and sold several houses.

His biggest undertaking was the acquisition of a magnificent area, where he built, with his own resources, a hotel-resort in Águas de São Pedro, in the interior of São Paulo.

## An obstinate doctor

Let us now see the story of Alfredo Heliton de Lemos, born in the interior of Pernambuco. At the age of 12, Heliton accepted the invitation to leave the interior of the Northeast and go to live with his brother in Rio de Janeiro.

Heliton did not go to live in Copacabana or Ipanema; he went to live with his brother in a slum, without guidance, affection or support from father and mother. In his new world, crime, drugs and prostitution surrounded him on all sides. Heliton recalls that sometimes what separated him from a shootout was just the walls of the shack where he lived.

Once, a friend who esteemed him very much decided to give him a gift. The friend asked him to close his eyes and open his hand. When Heliton opened his eyes, he saw in his hand the keys to anewly stolen car of the year. Your friend just said to him, "This is yours. When you can, you repay me ".

With a lot of effort, in order not to hurt his friend's feelings, he ended up convincing him that he couldn't accept the gift. When pondering about the environment in which he lived, young Heliton read one day that it was possible to be in the world and not be of the world. For this reason, despite living in an environment surrounded by evil, he obtained the strength to envision a better life, focused on virtue.

Once he was in a park, on a sunny afternoon, watching the effort of a beautiful heron trying to feed in the middle of a mire. It moved slowly, to prevent the mud from smearing its clear white feathers. That day, the poor young man from the hinterland pondered: "I am like that heron, which makes a great effort to survive without leaving me stained by the mud around me".

He then decided to replace the coexistence of colleagues and the "security" that he enjoyed among the hill bosses with experience and the discipline of his military career. At the age of 18, he joined the Army and also decided to reveal to the world his secret desire to one day become a doctor. He said with great pride and conviction to his colleagues: "Medicine is in me".

In uniform during the day, he fulfilled his military obligation. At night, I went to school to prepare for the entrance exam. He studied for a year to take his first medical exam, but he failed. Even so, his desire to become a doctor has not diminished. He studied for another year, took his second entrance exam and failed again.

Despite the difficulties he faced in his studies, the young man was persevering. Another year was prepared. He took his third entrance exam and failed again. Without being shaken by the three consecutive failures and moved by his deep desire to become a doctor, Heliton continued preparing for another year, to fail his fourth attempt.

At that time, he had already passed biology and veterinary, but that did not encourage him, because, despite failing four times, the student insisted on being a doctor. He studied another year and failed for the fifth time. He tried the entrance exam again and, when all his colleagues thought that this northeasterner was not born for medicine, Heliton was approved for the medical course at the Federal University of Rio de Janeiro. He entered college and continued his military career.

After graduation as a doctor, he completed his residency and specialized in ophthalmology. At the age of 32, he started practicing medicine. Soon he set up his office and the patients began to arrive. There were consultations, treatments for myopia, cataracts, strabismus, emergencies, surgeries, transplants ... Patients traveled long distances to be treated and medicated by their hands. Soon Dr. Heliton's name was respected in his midst. Over the years, he participated in several congresses in Brazil and abroad. Later, he acquired the necessary equipment and set up his own clinic. The years passed and Dr. Heliton, already retired in the post of colonel in the Army, was awarded a scholarship to spend two years at the University of Utah, in the United States, with expenses paid for him, his wife and the five children.The difference is not in the profession, but in the professional

Among hundreds of existing professions, it doesn't matter which one you choose. There is no one that is higher or lower, more noble or less important, more profitable or less rewarding than the other. What exists are professionals of superior quality, with a broader vision, bigger pretensions and higher dreams.

To illustrate this concept, think for a moment about how many gardeners you know. Maybe hundreds. How many gardeners do you know with the determination, determination and wisdom of businessman Norberto? Perhaps you can count them with the fingers of a single hand. How many students do you know who tried the entrance exam and failed? Maybe hundreds. How many students do you know who have had Dr. Heliton's perseverance and discipline? Again, you may be able to count them with the fingers of a single hand.

The difference lies within each one, in the willingness to overcome barriers and obstacles, to overcome their limits, to overcome themselves and in the intensity of the desire to win within each one.

Someone may say, "But some are smarter than others!" When I was a child, I used to think that some people were born smarter, more gifted, more prepared than others. This is a mistake, no one is born smarter than another. It is the individual who develops his intelligence throughout life, based on the decisions he makes in his daily life.

You can be as smart as the smartest person you know, as long as you apply yourself to a self-improvement discipline and exercise your mental faculties to overcome each of your limitations. Thus, we see that the university was not reserved only for children of wealthy parents, neither gardeners were destined to live a life of deprivation or need.

So, no matter what your profession, you will only achieve full success if you are willing to stand out for the excellence of a superior job.

So make the most of what you know and like to do. Resolve to make your talents a great contribution to humanity. Remember that the skills you admire in other people are acquired skills.

You can also acquire them, if you wish, after all, nobody is born singing, dancing, flying, flying, selling, teaching, managing or being successful. Instead, we are all born the same way: crying, however, as we grow up, we have the opportunity to create our world and choose what we want to be, have and do.

However, the choice is yours. If you don't decide for yourself, nobody will decide for you. Remember that the greatest privilege that God granted you in this lifetime was the gift of free will or the gift of free choice, that is, the freedom to do what you want in your life.

# Turn your talents into dollar signs

Your professional security will certainly come from your ability to transform your own talent, personal ability or natural gift into a source of income. When he succeeds in turning the talents that God has given him into currency, his work will no longer be monotonous, tiring, exhausting, intolerable, unbearable. Your work will become a source of pleasure, satisfaction and fulfillment.

Thomas Alva Edison, one of the greatest inventors of all times, was once asked how he managed to spend so many hours working in his laboratory. Your answer inspires us all. He said he didn't really work, but he spent his days entertaining and amusing. When he got tired of his challenging and pleasurable activities, he returned home.

Here is one of the secrets of a professionally successful person: developing a career in what brings you pleasure, a profession that is a distraction, an entertainment, a personal achievement and capable of generating a satisfactory income.

When you do a job you enjoy, it is no sacrifice to work long hours. For this reason, you have an obligation to yourself for your happiness: to find a job in which you fully fulfill yourself. Napoleon Hill stated:

The individual who does what he loves to do is rewarded with two prizes: first, because the work itself brings him a great feeling of happiness, which is priceless. Second, their financial returns, when spread over a lifetime of effort, are in general much higher in volume and better in quality, when compared to those performed by other interests.

No matter your area of professional or business interest, remember that you were born with a vocation. You are endowed with exclusive skills, gifts and talents. These gifts are yours, they are unique, no one can take them away from you. On the other hand, no one can develop them for you. The moment you succeed in turning the natural gifts that God has given you into currency, you will transform your work into a source of pleasure, satisfaction and fulfillment. That way, you will become a healthier, richer and much happier person.

## A formula for success

I notice that professionals in general feel very talented, educated and competent. Some are very qualified academically and are proud of their great "potential". They have an enviable curriculum, full of courses, postgraduate courses, master's degrees, and even the coveted MBA abroad. Some, however, have not yet learned to multiply their talents and convert them into currency.

There are others who have always wanted to own their own business, but do not know where to start. And there are also those who have already ventured out on a solo flight, but without the necessary structure, experience and support, they failed and ended up losing their savings, hope and self-esteem.

There are also those who have already won in the corporate world and now seek entrepreneurship for new challenges in a safe, healthy and stimulating environment. For people who are in that moment of life, I usually recommend the franchising system as the ideal option for their personal, professional and financial growth.

After 25 years of experience in this sector, I consider myself a real lover of the franchise system. In my opinion, this is the safest and most profitable way to open your own business. Statistics indicate that 80% of companies open in Brazil close their doors in the first years. In the franchise sector, 90% of businesses pass the initial mortality stage and perpetuate themselves as a successful business. The explanation for this surprising phenomenon is the fact that the individual uses a brand with national reputation, with a line of products and services already developed, with constant training programs, and all of this, combined with the transfer of management know-how and campaigns. high-level advertising to promote the business on a large scale.

With all these incentives, it is no wonder that in the past five years we have trained so many new millionaires. These emerging winners are optimistic, courageous, bold, extremely dynamic and have a drive that strongly propels them to achieve great achievements. They are entrepreneurs motivated by the spirit of serving the customer with promptness, excellence and joy. They bet on the education segment, believed in themselves and are reaping the fruit of their own investment.

They are people who take advantage of the fact that Brazil is experiencing its best moment of economic stability in recent years, with an emerging class of approximately 40 million new consumers with resources in their pockets and eager to acquire new products and services. Our economy is moving at an accelerated pace to occupy the fifth position in the world.

When a country experiences a moment of prosperity, fortunes change hands. With all this wealth in our country, it is no wonder that, every day, thirty new Brazilian millionaires emerge around us. And, sincerely, I hope that soon you will be part of this select group of new Brazilian millionaires!

**To awaken the millionaire in you, remember:**

Transform your natural gift into a source of income.

Develop a career in what brings you pleasure.

Multiply your earnings through a large-scale distribution channel.

**Mentalize:**

I am capable and intelligent.

I have a valuable vocation.

I have unique skills and abilities.

# Chapter 13

# Your dream has begun

The life is too short. Don't risk spending your days just tuning your instrument, without ever making a big show.

Do not condition your happiness to any future event. Some are deluded, thinking that they will only be happy after graduation, after marriage, after they get that promotion, after they buy a new car, after their children grow up, after their grandchildren come, after they retire.

Some hope to find happiness only after they leave this life. If you expect to find happiness when you are totally free from worries, doubts and adversity, rest assured that that day will never come.

So, start making your life what you have always dreamed of: it can be finding your loved one, restarting a loving relationship, building an empire, bringing children into the world, being healthier, recovering emotionally, regaining self-esteem and self-love, achieving peace of mind. No matter what it is, your dream should bring you an intimate feeling of following a destiny, of having a purpose, as if your life is a mission to be accomplished.

Turn your dream into a cause, so that you will have an extra reason to donate, to surrender to it. This cause should involve your personal development and the growth of other people.

A cause is something bigger than yourself. With this vision, you will have more inner strength to resist discouragement and the normal adversities encountered along the way. The value of the cause is greater than the value of an enterprise, because a true cause will continue for a long time, even after we have left this earthly existence.

So, commit yourself to living your millionaire dream.

# Promise yourself

## Promise to beat yourself physically.

Think of the gymnastics that your idol does daily to keep fit. If you're not a celebrity, you don't have to do the same. Just control your daily diet and undergo a regular exercise program. Walking is still the best way to exercise.

*Promise to beat yourself emotionally.* Control your emotions and your reactions in the face of adversity. Take a deep breath, count to ten. Control your environment. Do not allow the environment to control you.

*Promise to beat yourself in attitudes.* Your dynamism, positivism and enthusiasm will be the greatest tools for your achievements. Your attitude on a daily basis will determine your altitude in the climb of life.

*Promise to beat yourself in action.* Planning is good. Getting organized is recommended, but be firm when it comes to running. Don't be afraid to make mistakes. Worse than making mistakes is not trying. So, above all, do it.

*Promise to beat yourself in the discipline.* Sow thoughts and reap actions; sow actions and reap habits; sow habits and reap a character; sow a character and reap an eternal destiny.

*Promise to beat yourself in principle.* You will only achieve lasting success if your actions are governed by dignified, upright and just principles.

*Promise to beat yourself professionally.* Decide to do what you like, what gives you pleasure, what will eventually bring you recognition and a satisfactory financial return.

*Promise to beat yourself financially.* More important than winning is knowing how to save money. Develop a habit of regularly saving part of what you earn. After all, to accumulate 100 reais, you must first save 10 reais. To obtain 1,000 reais, you must first save 100 reais. And so on.

*Promise to beat yourself mentally*. As an architect of your destiny, use the mortar of good thoughts to build the masterpiece of your life. Get used to nurturing high, noble and uplifting thoughts. A good reading will help you a lot in this goal.

*Promise to beat yourself spiritually*. Try to discover the purpose of your life, live in communion with the Creator, receive divine guidance and live a life of faith.

## Happiness is a choice

To be happy, you don't have to be the greatest artist, scientist, athlete or the greatest entrepreneur in the world. An individual can be happy working in the field, taking care of the harvest and the animals.

Beauty, like happiness, is in the eye of the beholder. Thus, happiness is found by those who seek it in the simple details of each day. As Abraham Lincoln said, "A person is as happy as he sets out to be."

So, don't expect to be happy in a future time, after you have fulfilled all your dreams. Happiness is not in a destination

end, but on a daily basis, along the way.

Like all moods, happiness is a choice. So, choose to be happy today. This seems to be the secret of those who maintain their youth, regardless of their chronological age.

Remember that your biggest dream is to find happiness, but true happiness is found in the immense territories of the soul, where all the money in the world is worthless.

Many people seek to achieve fame, money, status and power as the most important goal in life. Don't forget, however, that happiness and money are not synonymous. There are many millionaires defeated and there are many successful individuals who do not have a fortune.

## Your greatest fortune

Journalists often ask me: How big is your fortune? When that happens, I take my phone out of my pocket and show him my family photo. This is my biggest fortune.

Life was made for man and not man for life. It was never intended to end his life just by working, losing his own personality in the midst of the search for material goods, recognition, power or fame.

So don't live to work, but work to live. After all, what's the use of you being the richest man in the world in a cemetery?

Logan Pearson Smith said: "There are two goals to be achieved in life. First, get what you want. Second, enjoy what has been achieved. Only the wisest perform the second".

Life is just a drop in the ocean from the immense perspective of eternity. There is nothing more extraordinary than being alive and enjoying this world full of emotions, adventures and progress.

# A possible dream

Life itself is already a big dream. So, as you move towards the realization of your great endeavors, whatever they may be, try to live a possible dream every day.

Try to understand yourself better, because that way you will better understand the world in which you live. Accept yourself fully, that way you will know how to accept the people around you.

Take better care of yourself, so you will be better able to take care of your fellowmen.

Be patient and tolerant of yourself and the people around you, as you will understand that everyone has their limitations and sometimes errs unconsciously or involuntarily.

Try to praise before criticizing someone, because, for each defect, the human being has ten virtues.

Greet yourself in the morning with joy, enthusiasm and a smile, in this way, you will transmit joy and enthusiasm in all your relationships.

Express, in words, the affection, esteem and admiration you feel for the people you love, as they are the most important in the world for you.

Thank the Creator for the countless blessings you receive and even for the blessings that you are unable to perceive or understand that He gives you.

Love yourself and your fellow men, for in this way you will be fulfilling the Creator's design.

In doing so, you will be fulfilling the greatest dream of all: being happy every day.

Go ahead, celebrating the gift of life, guided by the brilliance of the star itself, inspired by new horizons and scenarios that made it possible to awaken in you a new millionaire to make this world a better world.

**To awaken the millionaire in you, remember:**

Accept yourself fully.

Take better care of yourself.

Love yourself.

**Mentalize:**

I choose to be happy.

My greatest fortune is my family.

The time to live my dreams is now.

Made in United States
Troutdale, OR
12/12/2024